FIRST IMPRESSIONS

CREATING **WOW EXPERIENCES** IN YOUR CHURCH

MARK WALTZ

Loveland, Colorado
group.com

Group resources really work!

This Group resource incorporates our R.E.A.L. approach to ministry. It reinforces a growing friendship with Jesus, encourages long-term learning, and results in life transformation, because it's:

Relational—Learner-to-learner interaction enhances learning and builds Christian friendships.

Experiential—What learners experience through discussion and action sticks with them up to 9 times longer than what they simply hear or read.

Applicable—The aim of Christian education is to equip learners to be both hearers and doers of God's Word.

Learner-based—Learners understand and retain more when the learning process takes into consideration how they learn best.

Contents

Dedication and Acknowledgments 6

Introduction 7

Chapter 1: Reflections of a Consumer 11

Chapter 2: When Satisfaction's Not Enough 25

Chapter 3: Company's Coming. Are You Ready to Wow Them? 39

Chapter 4: Creating the "Wow!" Experience From the Outside In ...55

Chapter 5: The Hospitality Factor 71

Chapter 6: Service Behind the Scenes..............................81

Chapter 7: Training for the Experience 93

Chapter 8: Printed Impressions: Reading Between the Lines 109

Chapter 9: Beyond the Weekend 119

Chapter 10: Wow-Busters... 129

Epilogue: Lasting Impressions....................................... 143

Foreword

Our culture is caught up in the gaminess of first impressions. Personal image management—concerned with how people perceive us and accept us—drives us to obsession with first impressions. We want others to accept us. We want the confidence that comes from personal identity and value. Yet, peel back the layers and the smile often conceals the sadness, the up-to-the-minute fashion hides the lack of fulfillment, and the smooth talking drowns out the honest confession of confusion and brokenness.

At the same time, our society has become jaded and skeptical about trumped-up first impressions. People crave authentic relationships. They hunger for the satisfaction of acceptance. Everyone longs to know that their story, their personal and often confusing story, matters...to someone, anyone.

The truth is every individual story really does matter. And our stories are only understood fully inside the wonder and mystery of God's grand story. Connecting people—to the story of God and to the stories of others—is what the church is all about.

Creating "Wow!" experiences in your church is not an exercise in trumped-up first impressions to demonstrate how "impressive" your church is. Rather, authentic first impressions are about creating environments that allow us to meet people right where they are. First impressions are about communicating personal value, about expressing grace and acceptance. First impressions are about engaging personal stories in such a way that people are open to experience their story *inside* God's transforming story. His upper story is not merely about getting people through the rough places they find themselves; it is about something eternal. It is about doing life together in God's masterpiece of a story.

God's story is nothing less than impressive. His story elicits a "Wow!" God's people must elevate the wonder, the grandeur, and the excellence of God's story by creating cultures and environments that point to and celebrate his story. Creating "Wow!" experiences in your church is not an option. Being intentional about dynamic first impressions is to be true to God's story.

In this work Mark has done a masterful job describing practical details that help local churches do just that. This book will motivate you and your teams to help your guests feel welcome, safe, and accepted—*so that* they experience the grace of Jesus. We've unpacked this guide at Oak Hills Church. We've had Mark onsite to evaluate and make recommendations that have helped us improve our connection to our guests. I believe in Mark and what he has written.

Read this book. Discuss it with your leaders and teams. Then apply it. You'll be impressed.

Randy Frazee
Senior Minister
Oak Hills Church, San Antonio, Texas

Dedication

To the guest services ministry volunteers at Granger Community Church who say to every guest on every campus, "You matter to God." This is your story. The Granger model of welcome and grace is yours. You've created it, embraced it, and lived it out. Thank you for allowing me the privilege of serving beside you. I am amazed at your love for Jesus and your care for those who matter to him. This work is dedicated to each of you.

Acknowledgments

The thrill of living is found in sharing the adventure with others. I'd like to thank the following people for their support of my life and ministry development.

- Laura, my best friend, my lover, and my life partner, you define *wife*. You've been my sounding board, my cheerleader, and my prayer supporter. I experience the character of God in your grace. You are my treasure.
- Olivia, your creativity keeps me active, and your energy keeps me young. I'm so grateful to be your dad.
- Mark Beeson, I have been captivated by your vision, inspired by your leadership, and challenged by your integrity. I am honored to run after the vision God has called you—and now me—to fulfill.
- Tim Stevens, Jason Miller, Kem Meyer, and Rob Wegner, who also make up the senior management team at Granger, what a ride! You challenge me, encourage me, and laugh hard with me. I value our friendship on the journey.
- Rusty Carlson, you've answered my midnight calls, extended grace when I'd forgotten what it was, and been a faithful friend over the years and the miles.
- Dad and Mom, thank you for introducing me to Jesus and teaching me that first impressions matter because people matter.
- My heartfelt thanks to those who reviewed my early manuscripts and contained their laughter: Donna Waltz, Franco Zizzo, Ginny Lawley, John White, Kem Meyer, Laura Waltz, Nancy Lankerd, Rusty Carlson, Susan Chipman, Tim Stevens, and Vicki Martin.
- To my editor, Bob D'Ambrosio, and the team at Group Publishing, thank you for your trust and partnership to help resource other churches.

Introduction

"And whatever you do, do it heartily."
(Colossians 3:23a, New King James Version)

"There's no such thing as an artificial experience."[1]

When my publisher asked me to consider editing this work for a re-release, I thought it was a good idea. A lot has changed in our culture since its first release in 2005. Few of us print maps to navigate a journey; we have voice-activated GPS apps on our phones. Not many churches are producing DVDs anymore; downloadable or on-demand options allow most of us to watch a service or access training online. It was true—the book needed an update.

But plenty has changed around our local church, Granger Community Church, since 2005. Our executive pastor, Tim Stevens, documented our painful journey and ultimate renewed life in his book *"Vision: Lost and Found: The Story of a Church That Got Stuck But Didn't Stay There."* You can read the full story in his book. I'll bottom line it with this: We emerged with a five-year vision through 2016 that turned our ministry upside down.

Challenged with what it means to follow Jesus where Jesus goes, struck with the hard-hitting picture of what it is to be the Church from the book of Acts, and faced with the reality that a growing number of our population will not be drawn to the way we "do church," we wrestled with our entire approach to ministry as the local church. Our new vision shook us to our core. It was bigger than anything we'd ever dreamed before (God-sized). It was focused outside our church walls as well as within (paradigm-shifting). And it challenged every individual, not just our corporate body (convicting).

I've always taught that this ministry of guest services—making indelible first impressions—was a matter of our heart, but this new vision wakened something inside me that changed how I would lead, coach, and write about first impressions. If ministry is ministry whether it happens on Sunday in a church building or on Monday in an office, then people are people who matter to God whether they are in our church building or at our workplace.

First impressions aren't about making the institution look good. They are about making Jesus look good. They are about communicating personal value to the people who matter to him.

Does the server who screws up my meal on Friday night have personal value then or only on Sunday when she walks through the doors of our church? Does my neighbor matter to God when his dog barks until 2 a.m., keeping me awake, or does he only matter when he attends our church service?

The value of first impressions around our weekend services, youth events, children's programming, and mid-week activities hasn't been minimized through our fresh vision to reach people where they are (even if they're not at our church building); it has, rather, been elevated to an all-new level of critical importance.

Our guests and yours want to experience people who are real. Genuine. Authentic. People who live what they say they believe. People who act like other people actually matter. They want to see that in our workplace, at the gym, over the neighborhood fence, and in our church.

First impressions really matter. I think they have eternal weight. People will either first be impressed with our Jesus-way love toward them...or they won't. This is a big deal.

I'll repeat the story I wrote about in this book's first release. It still captures the critical nature of first impressions and celebrates the Gospel when we get it right.

It's the story of a woman who visited our Granger campus some time ago. A devout Jew, she had been investigating the claims of Christ through a small group in Chicago. After a year of conversation with this little group of Christ followers, she still had not decided to accept that Jesus is the Messiah, the way home to her Father.

When she traveled to our area to visit her extended family, they invited her to join them for a service at our church, which they had been checking out. She agreed to go, but then a family argument broke out, and she left without intending to go to church at all that weekend. As she was driving out of town, she passed our church and decided to attend a service with her three young children.

She found the parking lot volunteer, John, to be warm and genuinely interested in her and her family. When she entered our church building, she was met by a member of our hospitality team, who provided a tour and helped her get her children settled in the appropriate rooms. By the time she entered the service, she wasn't thinking about the dispute with her family anymore, and every word in the message seemed to be intended just for her.

As she stepped out of the service, she was greeted by John, from the parking lot, who introduced his wife, Nancy. They helped her with her children and offered to answer her questions.

Now here's the power of first impressions offered in the love of Jesus.

She returned to Chicago and announced to her new friends, "OK, now I'm ready to receive Jesus Christ as my Savior. The love and grace I experienced from that parking lot helper and the greeter were all I needed. I'm in."

That's what this book is about. That's what our ministry of guest services is about.

At Granger Community Church, we've developed our entire guest services ministry around this reality. The people serving on our guest services teams have one focus: creating experiences that bring guests back to our church services. When guests are valued, they will return. And every time they return, they'll have the opportunity to experience Jesus' love through our teams and our message. On each of our campuses at Granger, we strive to make first impressions that demonstrate that all people are significant to God and to us.

This book will help you develop a similar ministry focus within your church. It will help you

- understand your guests as real people with real needs;
- develop a ministry to your guests that communicates acceptance, respect, and value;
- build teams who believe that people matter to God; and
- honor God as you offer your best to your people and community.

Throughout the book, you'll find references to Granger Community Church, where I lead our connections and multisite ministries. These references to our ministry approach are offered as examples. Our campuses range in attendance from a few hundred to several thousand each weekend. Some sites are portable, some are small church buildings, and our Granger campus covers 52 acres. The principles are the same, and they are scalable. *Your* approach will be different because your local church's environment is not the same as ours. I've also included examples from a variety of businesses and other churches. If any of them inspire an idea for ministry that is relevant to your setting—great! However, I encourage you to apply *principles and concepts* to help you shape a unique ministry that brings guests back to *your* church.

You'll find exercises sprinkled throughout the book, as well as review questions at the end of each chapter. Consider them privately, or use them to spark conversation among your board or team members. I've included some exercises that may be helpful in structuring, training, and evaluating your teams; feel free to revise them to best fit your ministry culture. Use this book as a guide to help you tap the resources that God has already planted within your church.

Ultimately, as you take steps to enhance first impressions in your church, your guests will be impressed with God. As you and your church create experiences that say "You matter to God—therefore you matter to us," your guests will be drawn to Jesus, and you will have served him well.

Endnote

1. B. Joseph Pine II and James H. Gilmore, *The Experience Economy* (Boston: Harvard Business School Press, 1999), 37.

Reflections of a Consumer

---

*"The customer only wants two things—
show me you care about me personally, and
tell me what you're going to do for me now
(help me—please)."*[1]

Defining the Consumer

I'm sitting in Starbucks, and I love it. My hazelnut coffee is steaming next to my laptop. The rich aroma of espresso beans fills the air. Conversations from faithful patrons are creating a buzz of community in the room.

I'm not the only one at work in my portable office. A young college student is kicking out a term paper. Across the room two women enjoy a slice of cheesecake, interspersed with dialogue about their kids. An older couple sits quietly, sipping coffee, each person engrossed in a magazine. I'm surrounded by people in diverse stages of life: married people, divorced people, new parents, students, retired folks.

My dictionary defines *consumer* this way: "a person who consumes; buys goods and services for personal needs." Whatever else the people around me are doing, they are consuming, and so am I.

Consumerism and the Local Church

The word *consumer* can be offensive when used in relationship to the local church. Consumerism is one thing at Starbucks, but it seems to have no place in the local church. We appropriately object to the notion of setting up our churches as marketplaces, selling our Jesus wares, and catering to every selfish whim of the people who enter our doors. A consumer mentality—wherein I am the central figure in the universe, the church exists to tell me what I want to hear, and God is a materialistic vending machine to satisfy my every desire—is not reflective of the character of Jesus Christ. The church is not called to be the catering, whim-granting marketplace of the 21st century.

Nonetheless, I am a consumer. So are you. So is every individual who enters your church. What are the ramifications of this fact for the church?

There's a Consumer in Your Mirror

Consider the consumer role you play. Think about your daily needs, your leisure, your business. Where do you shop? Where do you conduct business? Where do you bank? Where are your clothes cleaned? Where do you buy groceries? Where do you eat? On which airlines do you fly? What hotels do you frequent?

If you were to pull out your receipts from the past six months, you'd likely see some patterns. Why do you frequent the same places week after week? Value? Customer service? Consistency?

Where Do You Consume?

Make a short list. Where do you shop? Who provides service for you? Jot down ten places you frequent as a consumer.

_____

_____

_____

_____

_____

_____

Complete the exercise to the left. What businesses did you list? Underline the ones you visit often or even exclusively. For each of those, cite one or more reasons you return again and again. You may shop at your supermarket for value, while quality takes you back to your mechanic. You may love shopping at a particular clothing store—physically or online—because of service and quality. Whatever you identify as the reason to return, you have established expectations of each vendor.

When Is Adequate Not Enough?

Our expectations communicate a lot about what we value. When we dine out, we expect the food to be warm, the drinks to be cold, and the service to be swift. We want our server to be personable, courteous, and conscientious. We expect the check to reflect the value not only of our meal but also of our overall dining experience.

That's why we'll eat at a fast-food diner with laminated tabletops, cheap prints on the wall, and a self-serve soda fountain. The value of our experience is reflected in the check. It doesn't cost us much. It satisfies our hunger. It's adequate.

Adequate defines many of our experiences, doesn't it? A trip to the mall, a sandwich for lunch, and a transaction at the bank are generally adequate experiences. Adequate isn't *bad*. We get what we need. The experience just isn't anything to write home about. It isn't *memorable*.

But often we expect more than adequate. We want to experience a memory-maker now and then. And when we do, a new standard has been set. We know excellence *can* be delivered. We know we *can* find a better value. Often we settle for adequate…but we know that excellence *is* possible.

Several years ago, my wife and I were invited by her employer at that time to an evening at an upscale restaurant in LaPorte, Indiana. Our dining experience there redefined our standard of excellence.

The environment was eclectic and welcoming. The charm of the room whispered "intimate," while the bright yellow paint splashed on the 20-foot walls shouted "fun." Swing jazz, playing seductively in the background, set a New Orleans mood, right for good times and great friends.

Our tables, every place setting arranged perfectly, were adorned with rare meadow flowers (a far cry from those little silk daisies cemented in clear glue). Each course was beautifully presented and delicious. The hors d'oeuvres were delectable and plentiful. It was by far the best meal my wife and I had ever tasted. Throughout the meal our server called each of us by name. This was more than a distinctive meal; this was an event.

This exceptional experience recalibrated my expectations of restaurants. Now I know what's possible. Every other restaurant will pale in comparison to this one.

Consumers' expectations aren't restricted to dining. We expect our family doctors to be on time. (OK, we really don't, which is why their perpetual delay ticks us off so much—we know it's possible to be on time!) We expect our flights to be on time, our mail carriers to follow consistent delivery schedules, and our work associates to arrive as scheduled. We expect Wi-Fi to be available for research and e-mail; we expect our elected officials to represent our best interests; we expect our favorite clothing stores to have the styles we want in the colors and sizes we need.

Too often, though, we have to settle for adequate. If the meal is at least warm, we'll eat it. If the wait at the post office isn't too long, we'll endure it. If the doctor will make an accurate diagnosis, we'll wait. We'll settle for adequate, but we long for more.

From Adequate to "Wow!"

What my wife and I experienced at the upscale restaurant was "Wow!"— something way beyond our expectations and certainly far more than adequate. Someone went beyond the norm to communicate caring and to create a truly memorable experience.

What Are Your "Wow!" Moments? Recall two or three times you've been wowed. Who blew you away with excellent service? Who surprised you with remarkably good quality? Who impressed you with a product's value? What did the people involved in these experiences do? How did their actions and behavior affect you?

_____

_____

_____

When was the last time you had a "Wow!" experience? For most of us, these moments are few and far between. It takes a lot for us to be impressed; it takes even more for us to be wowed.

We consumers don't merely evaluate _what_ we consume; we evaluate the entire experience. When thinking about past "Wow!" experiences, we see faces, hear voices and other ambient sounds, remember smells, and recall emotions. All five senses may have been engaged. The fantastic restaurant experience I described included décor, music, food presentation, taste, and service. But more than anything, it was about people and the way they treated us. When we feel personally valued in a particular setting, we'll likely return.

The opposite is also true. We'll think twice about returning to a place in which we felt marginalized or devalued.

One Friday evening I took my family to a popular national grill. Liv, our daughter, ordered a quesadilla meal, complete with sour cream and guacamole. Excited about her selection, she picked up her fork to lavish sour cream onto her first bite of quesadilla. Suddenly she dropped her fork and jumped away from the table, exclaiming, "Yuck! There's a hair!" Well, it certainly wasn't the first time my wife or I had seen a hair in a plate of food, but what happened next did surprise us.

We requested a new dollop of sour cream—twice. And each time a hair accompanied the condiment. Are you counting? We did! That was three servings of sour cream, each time with a hair from the kitchen! Liv was done, finished. She was ready to leave and never visit the restaurant again.

We politely asked for a different plate of food, hoping our server wouldn't charge us for Olivia's meal at all. When the substandard service was not followed up with any demonstration of responsibility, we left, knowing it would be a while before we returned—if ever.

Beyond unmet expectations, we didn't feel valued. We weren't made to feel we mattered. The staff gave no consideration to the fact that we might not return or that we might tell others about our experience.

On the other hand, businesses that intentionally communicate a caring attitude have won my respect and repeat business. I'm not a world traveler, but over the years, DoubleTree hotels and suites have impressed me with the warm chocolate chip cookies that are given to guests upon check-in. (Here's a company that understands the importance of little things!) When my family and I dine at our favorite local Mexican restaurant, we hope Bill is working. He sees that our drinks are fresh and warmly stops by our table to chat. His excellence earns return trips from us and rewarding tips for him. The online travel people at Hotwire.com surprised me when their representative didn't say no to my request but said instead, "That's a really good idea; I'll note it as a customer enhancement proposal." The barista at our local Starbucks knew my name and drink. I'll keep going back to these places because they've communicated that they value me.

The same is true of guests in our churches. The churches delivering experiences that exceed guests' expectations are those to which people return, again and again, until they're no longer guests but full-fledged members of the church community. When a guest thinks "Wow!" it is because he or she feels affirmed and valued. The church has said, "You matter."

Accepting Consumers in Your Church

You may be thinking, "Yes, but responding to our guests as consumers is catering to their base wants and whims. As Christians we should be calling them to a higher standard of integrity and commitment, away from self-focused consumerism. When we see our guests as consumers, we reinforce their self-centered lifestyle. The local church is not about catering to the cultural expectations established in the marketplace; the church's job is to lift up Jesus so seekers can see him."

> Our goal should be to do anything and everything that helps our guests see Christ.

I agree. Our assignment is to make sure people can see Jesus clearly. This is the very reason we must meet them where they are—consumer mentality and all. We must greet them with unconditional acceptance and respect. This is how people will begin to see Jesus clearly. Our goal should be to do anything and everything that helps our guests see Christ.

Since the inception of Granger Community Church, a prominent core value has been "People matter to God; therefore, they matter to us." Mark Beeson, our senior pastor, communicates that he values every attendee in our church. Every time Mark speaks, his listeners hear how much they matter to God. Because he has cast this vision so well, dozens of teams of people help communicate this core value every weekend. Hundreds of us have caught this vision to reach out to people who need the hope of Jesus in a world where few people really care about them. We've accepted that it's the only way to accomplish our mission: "helping people take their next step toward Christ…together."

How do you view first-time guests in your church, particularly those guests who are seeking God—again or for the first time in their lives? What labels have you attached to them? "Nonbelievers"? "Unchurched"? "Lost"? "Sinners"? Words like these are often used to describe people who are seeking—those who are searching for answers, exploring the claims of Christ, looking for hope in a hopeless world. But when we attach such labels to those who are not Christ-followers, we need to be aware of the nuances those labels carry with them. For instance, terms such as *sinners* and *visitors* have caused us to further alienate those who are really no different from ourselves; we're all on a spiritual journey in search of purpose and fulfillment.

On the other hand, terms such as *seekers* and *unconvinced* help us approach our guests with a message that is sensitive to their exploration and journey toward God. When we remember our guests are *seeking* and are *unconvinced*, we tear down invisible barriers and are able to more naturally communicate love and acceptance.

I suggest we remember that our seeking friends are also *consumers*. I know that such a label may seem too marketplace-oriented. Perhaps it sounds shallow, if not hollow, but it is honest. Those who seek—who decide to "try church again," to explore the claims of Christ in relationship to their lives—are "shopping" for a church. More important, they are shopping for a spiritual *experience* that addresses their personal needs. I propose we meet them right where they are: at our doors, shopping for help in life, full of expectations, hoping someone will care for them.

Jesus and Consumerism

I still see "WWJD" printed on bumper stickers, wristbands, charms, and Bible covers, encouraging us to continually ask ourselves, "What would Jesus do?" Let's consider how Jesus encountered consumerism in his day, and rather than asking what he *would* do, let's consider what he *did*.

Read this account of one of Jesus' miracles, as described in Mark 6:34-44.

When Jesus landed and saw a large crowd, he had compassion on them, because they were like sheep without a shepherd. So he began teaching them many things. By this time it was late in the day, so his disciples came to him. "This is a remote place," they said, "and it's already very late. Send the people away so they can go to the surrounding countryside and villages and buy themselves something to eat."

But he answered, "You give them something to eat."

They said to him, "That would take eight months of a man's wages! Are we to go and spend that much on bread and give it to them to eat?"

"How many loaves do you have?" he asked. "Go and see."

When they found out, they said, "Five—and two fish."

Then Jesus directed them to have all the people sit down in groups on the green grass. So they sat down in groups of hundreds and fifties. Taking the five loaves and the two fish and looking up to heaven, he gave thanks and broke the loaves. Then he gave them to his disciples to set before the people. He also divided the two fish among them all. They all ate and were satisfied, and the disciples picked up twelve basketfuls of broken pieces of bread and fish. The number of the men who had eaten was five thousand.

Writing about this same event, the Gospel writer John describes a conversation in which Jesus confronted the motivation of his "consumer" crowd: "Jesus answered, 'You've come looking for me not because you saw God in my actions but because I fed you, filled your stomachs—and for free' " (John 6:26, The Message).

Before and after this open-air, impromptu banquet, people came to Jesus in search of healing for themselves, their families, and their friends. They wanted their own needs to be met. These crowds definitely fit our definition of *consumers*.

But here's the amazing thing: Jesus didn't stop healing or performing other miracles. He continued to play into the people's consumer mind-set. He did this because he wanted them to see the Father. He didn't seem too worried that their motives were self-serving.

When Jesus asked people to move from consumerism to commitment (John 6), some "followers" turned away. The same thing may happen when people in our churches are invited to embrace a personal relationship with Jesus and follow him by serving others. Even so, Jesus continued rolling out the red carpet and communicating this simple message: "Lost people matter to my Father; therefore, they matter to me." This must be the church's message today as well.

> In time, our guests' values will get sorted out inside a *personal relationship* with God. As this relationship develops, the materialistic consumerism that poses a threat to personal holiness and integrity will begin to melt away.

Is it possible that the church will somehow communicate a value system of consumerism that merely reflects the self-focused interests of our culture? Perhaps, but I believe it is worth the risk. Because in time, our guests' values will get sorted out inside a *personal relationship* with God. As this relationship develops, the materialistic consumerism that poses a threat to personal holiness and integrity will begin to melt away.

The people who come through your doors on the weekend are initially making decisions as consumers. Whether they return rests on their entire experience on your campus. They leave asking the same questions they ask of businesses throughout the week: "Was this worth my time? Do the people care about me? Am I valued here?" How will your guests answer these questions?

Competition You Never Asked For

Maybe you're thinking, "First you suggest we need to *cater* to consumers, and now you are talking about *competition*. I want my money back!"

I can appreciate this concern. After all, none of us decided to lead in a local church because we wanted to compete. This isn't *our* gig. It's God's.

> **Y**our competition, the rival that will keep people away from your church, is any business, service, or experience your guests have encountered in the past few weeks.

This is not about us; it's about him, his church, his people. It's him we offer to those who seek—not a program, not a celebrity preacher, not a mere experience. We offer Christ.

But because we live in a consumer environment, there *is* competition. There are winners and losers. If your church is going to be effective, then you must beat the competition, pure and simple. You must find out who the competition is, what it is doing, and how to win its consumers to your church. You must figure out how to convince potential guests why they should be at your church on Sunday morning.

OK, time out. Let me assure you I'm *not* saying other churches are our competition. As pastors and leaders, we're not attempting to beat out the other churches in town. We don't watch what other churches are doing so we can "top" them. No, the other Christ-centered churches in town are on our team. They are leading and loving for the same cause. They are arm-in-arm with our church, making a difference in our community.

If your biggest competition on Sunday morning isn't another church in town, then what is it? Your competition, the rival that will keep people away from your church, is any business, service, or experience your guests have encountered in the past few weeks. The competition includes restaurants, malls, golf courses, and amusement parks. First Bank (not First Church), United Parcel (not United Methodist), and Zappos (not Nazarenes) set the bar for service.

The competition doesn't happen only during weekend worship services. The competition for your guests began when they were wowed in another environment. One or more of your guests shipped a package to the other side of the country last week, assured it would arrive there by noon the next day. You have a guest who fired two people last month because they didn't make their sales quotas for the second month in the quarter. Another guest picked up his laundry at his local cleaner, pleased his shirts were treated with medium starch and ready in two days as promised. You have guests who are greeted by name at their local coffee shop and rewarded with free drinks because they are frequent shoppers. Even their discount supercenter provides special parking for pregnant moms and handicapped patrons. Your guests have high expectations that are formed every day from new encounters with excellence and conscientious care. Although too much of their world is merely adequate, they know

Will your guests' experience in your church be worth getting out of bed?

excellence, and they return to places where they experience it.

Finally, don't forget the profound competition of your guests' warm, cozy beds. After all, competition in the mind of the consumer is about the value of the experience. Will your guests' experience in your church be worth getting out of bed?

Competition for experiences that affirm the customer's value is so intense in today's culture that consumers often base the quality of any business— or church—on *the first few seconds of their experience.*

First Impressions Are Lasting Impressions

First impressions aren't limited to any single aspect of the guests' experience. The SuperAmerica company training program summarizes it this way: "From the customer's point of view, if they can see it, walk on it, hold it, hear it, step in it, smell it, carry it, step over it, touch it, use it, even taste it, if they can feel it or sense it, it's customer service."[2] That pretty much covers it. If it can be experienced, it's service—whether it's poor service or phenomenal service.

Additionally, service of any kind isn't merely about *first* impressions; it's about *lasting* impressions. Some of the impressions you've retained about a business (or church, for that matter) didn't come within the first few minutes of your experience; they occurred sometime later. But they remained.

Complete the exercise on page 22. Now evaluate the impressions you jotted down. Which reflect your feelings from your *initial* encounter, and which ones describe your thoughts at the *end* of your experience with that organization? What does this tell you about the impressions we retain?

First impressions in the local church are about creating the atmosphere expressed in Jesus' invitation to grace-filled community in Matthew 11:28-30.

As you review the few words you just recorded, you'll find a mixture of phrases that express not only your first impression but your *lasting* impression as well. These impressions will help you decide to return or to find another provider.

Organizations that understand the lasting nature of first impressions also understand that *people matter*. When people matter, guests are wowed. And when guests are wowed, they know they matter.

Consumers Are People, and People Need Relationships

In the end, an appropriate approach to consumerism is to see not consumers, but people—people who matter to God. The motivation to make a "Wow!" impression is not to better everyone else in town. It's not about stroking our egos, pleased with how excellent we are. "Wow!" impressions matter because people matter. What they think matters. What they believe matters. What they want matters. What they need matters.

First Impressions Last

Let's try this word-association exercise. Look at the following list, and jot down your first thought about each place. Don't spend a lot of time on this—just write the first thought that comes to mind.

McDonald's —————————————————

Your last hotel stay (not the name of the hotel, but your impression of it)

—————————————————

Your last airplane experience (again, not the name of the company)

—————————————————

Your bank —————————————————

Your local church —————————————————

Starbucks —————————————————

When our guests know they matter, we've connected with them on a human level. It's really the only place to connect. It's where Jesus connects with us.

First impressions in the local church are about creating the atmosphere expressed in Jesus' invitation to grace-filled community in Matthew 11:28-30:

> *Are you tired? Worn out? Burned out on religion? Come to me. Get away with me and you'll recover your life. I'll show you how to take a real rest. Walk with me and work with me—watch how I do it. Learn the unforced rhythms of grace. I won't lay anything heavy or ill-fitting on you. Keep company with me and you'll learn to live freely and lightly* (The Message*)*.

People matter to God, therefore they *must* matter to us. If we in the local church can faithfully follow Jesus' model in communicating this truth, the guests in our churches will experience acceptance and grace. They will know they are valued. They will observe authentic relationships and long to be part of them. It all begins with meeting people where they are.

Try These Next Steps...

- The next time you dine out, talk with your dinner guests about your shared experience. What disappointed you? Did the staff members do the best they could with what they had? What would have created a "Wow!" experience for you?

- At the end of your day or week, make a list of your consumer encounters. When did you feel valued? What did someone do or say that caught you by surprise in a positive way? When were you wowed? How could an aspect of this "Wow!" experience be duplicated in your church?

- Did you have the opportunity to show someone that you value him or her this week? What did you do? What could you have done better?

Endnotes

1. Jeffrey Gitomer, *Customer Satisfaction Is Worthless, Customer Loyalty Is Priceless* (Atlanta: Bard Press, 1998), 35.

2. As quoted in *Delivering Knock Your Socks Off Service* by Kristin Anderson and Ron Zemke (New York: American Management Association, 2003), 29.

2

When Satisfaction's Not Enough

"The bottom line of service is how you feel about a business as a result of having done a transaction, while experience is how you feel about yourself as the result of a transaction."[1]

Simple Distractions, Major Disappointments

On a flight home from Atlanta, my wife and I had an hour-long layover in Detroit. Before boarding we had ample time to make our way from one end of the airport to the other to arrange our seat assignments. Upon arriving at our concourse, we saw a long line already forming at a single station near our gate. In an effort to avoid a long, probably unnecessary wait, I headed down the gate corridor in search of a knowledgeable agent.

I saw an official-looking woman heading my way. I was happy. But she told me I had been in the right place; all gates were serviced at this one counter with the long, never-ending line. I was not happy.

We waited ten more minutes before another agent showed up. When I told her South Bend was our destination, she sent us to our gate, saying the personnel there would assign seats 30 minutes prior to boarding. This information was inconsistent with what I'd just been told, but it did get us out of the long line and to the gate. It sounded good to me.

While waiting at our gate, I overheard a *third* agent tell an inquiring passenger he'd have no trouble flying standby because the flight wasn't full. However, 35 minutes later, when we were finally at the podium to get our seat assignments and board, we were informed by a *fourth* agent, "Please step aside; this flight is overbooked."

I bit my tongue, hard. We stepped aside, annoyed and tired by the long lines and misinformation. We weren't even on the plane yet. We had experienced only a fraction of this airline's services. Although the flight might be smooth and the attendants might offer extraordinary service, it was too late. We were dissatisfied. Before we could be satisfied, we had to *not* be *dis*satisfied. The same is true of your guests on Sunday morning.

Identify Potential Distractions

When your guests are distracted from the real purpose of their visit to your church, you'll have a difficult time re-engaging them. In order for people to see Jesus, potential distractions *must* be identified and eliminated. Sometimes a simple look around can reveal a lot:

- There's only one roll of tissue in each restroom stall. What if the supply is depleted?

- The lobby is too congested for guests to find their way to the auditorium.

- The walk to the children's center is down four flights of stairs, and the auditorium is on the main level.

When we eliminate potential or obvious distractions, we can more nearly assure that our guests won't be dissatisfied. This must be done before they can be satisfied. Discovering what dissatisfies guests requires a fresh set of eyes.

Visit Your Church...Again

Laura, my wife, has always taken great pride in keeping our home clean and welcoming. But there's one exception: She absolutely hates to dust.

So dusting is my job. It seems like a reasonable request, considering how much she does throughout the week. Even though she asks that I dust only once a week, how many times a week do you suppose she has to remind me? She'd say, "Too many!"

I just forget. I don't see the dust. I set my drink on an end table and don't notice the dust bunnies. I watch television and look right through the layer of dust on the screen. In my home I'm in a familiar place, and I miss the obvious.

How familiar are you with your own church building and campus? All of us tend to grow comfortable with our surroundings, and we often don't see what our guests see. We park in the same parking space; we don't notice the cracks in the parking lot. We walk through the same front door; we don't see how dirty the glass is. We use the same restroom; we don't see the chipped tile. And even if we do notice these things, they are probably less important to us than they are to our guests.

We register guests and members for classes and events, but we don't see the complicated registration system that guests experience. We walk across the lobby carpet, but we don't see the stains anymore. We know where the restrooms are; we don't realize there are not enough signs to help first-time guests find them.

We need fresh eyes. We need the eyes of our first-time guests. It would be a good exercise to ask your guests what they saw and experienced during their first visit. You might also try to visit your church for the "first" time all over again. Slow down. Enter the parking lot asking, "Are the parking spaces visible?" Pay attention during your walk to the building. Do you have to wade through puddles that could be redirected? Do you walk over rough or dusty terrain? Consider the landscaping. Do weeds grow against the side of the building? Is trash caught beneath the shrubs and in corners? Are walkways dirty? How easy is it to find your way to the front entrance? to the restroom? to the auditorium? Are members of your greeting team situated in helpful places? Are they genuinely friendly and observant?

For most of us, it has been a long time since we experienced what our first-time guests encounter. We are the first ones to arrive and the last ones to leave. We never fight traffic or squeeze through the hallways with an arriving crowd. So this week, arrive at church when everyone else does. Drop your kids off in the nursery when all the other parents do. Try leaving the parking lot with everyone else after church.

A fresh look may reveal more than dust bunnies.

That reminds me...I have some dusting to do.

Be Your Next Guest

Plan a time within the month to experience your own church as a guest. Pay attention to the following areas:

- Parking (coming and going)—Note the effectiveness of signs (or lack of them), traffic flow, and specific trouble spots.

- The approach to the building—Look for overgrown landscaping and broken, worn, or dangerous steps and other elements. Scrutinize the terrain, signage, and entrances.

- The children's ministry area—Pay attention to the registration process, the friendliness and approachability of the children's workers, and your wait time.

- The attitude of the people around you—How are you feeling since your arrival on the campus?

Record your findings here or in a separate notebook, and discuss them with your team. What can be done right away to improve these first impressions? Prioritize your steps toward eliminating potential distractions.

_____

_____

_____

_____

_____

_____

_____

_____

Visit Someplace Else

A helpful exercise in retraining your senses is to evaluate an unfamiliar place. The next time you dine out, take a notebook with you and plan to do more than eat a meal. Be the critic. Record impressions about the parking area, the building, your host or hostess, wait time, service, food, and ambiance. How did you feel about the entire experience? What wowed you, if anything? The goal is not to see what you can find wrong, but rather to train yourself to see from a guest's perspective (after all, you are one).

Much can be learned from public establishments designed to accommodate high volumes of people. Airports, museums, and malls can be invaluable in helping you understand what your guests look for at your church. Even if your church is smaller in square footage, learning from experts in design and functionality will help you create an engaging environment.

For instance, I pay close attention to signage at airports. I get turned around rather easily, so when I enter the concourse on my way to a connecting flight, I need clear, visible directions to my next plane. With only twenty minutes to walk to the next gate, there's no time to waste.

When I go to a new mall, I pay attention to the atmosphere created by light, color, and shapes. I listen for music, water, and other background sounds. I evaluate placement and visibility of information centers, directory kiosks, and signs.

Visit other churches. It's much easier to evaluate aspects of a guest's experience at a church other than your own. You may go home grateful for your guest services ministry, or you may return with good ideas for improvements.

In my consulting, I assess information centers and guest services kiosks in other churches. I pay attention to signage, placement, sight lines, lighting, and personnel. I want to be helpful to these churches and the benefactor in my own.

I remember several years ago discovering how I had become familiar with our information kiosk, registration systems, and signage. I realized the words on the bulkhead over the information center read "Lower Level." It seemed ridiculous that for months I had missed such a glaring error.

The sign had been hung some time before the movable kiosk had been positioned a few feet in front of the staircase to the lower level. The sign marked the stairs, but our guests didn't know that. To fresh eyes it looked like a ticket booth to get to the lower level of the building. If I were a guest at our church, I wouldn't have stopped at the "Lower Level" desk!

More recently we opened new space and completed a sign audit. We re-signed everything with larger fonts and clear language.

So take a field trip. Visit an airport, museum, mall, or another church, and allow enough time to assess your experience as a guest. Use the "Be the Guest" worksheets on pages 37 and 38 to record your thoughts and perceptions. You may want to record your ideas directly in this book, or you may photocopy the worksheet for yourself and others on your team. Ask all the questions on the worksheet and more. Make specific notes, and talk with others about your experience. Then use this information to evaluate your church.

One final comment about identifying and removing distractions: Put yourself in the position of your guests and anticipate potential problems. Know what *could* go wrong, then prevent it. Of course, you won't be able to anticipate every distraction, but when you develop a pattern of excellence, your guests will offer grace when a distraction does occur.

The Power of Mission

There is no greater distraction than a church that doesn't have a stated and agreed-upon mission. At Granger, we want people to see Jesus. We want them to begin a personal relationship with Jesus and begin to live out his purposes for their lives. We don't want anything to distract from this objective. Our motivation is not to be big; it is to see as many people as possible come to faith in Christ. We view growth as a natural byproduct of meeting people where they are and inviting them to join us in our mission.

At Granger this mission is "helping people take their next step toward Christ…together." This motivates us to create a safe and welcoming environment for our guests. It drives us to meet people where they are, not where we wish they were. We are constantly developing a variety of environments to cultivate authentic relationships in which people can take one step at a time toward Christ. If anything gets in the way of helping people take their next step, we've failed.

What Is Your Mission?

If you've gotten this far in your reading and don't know your church's mission, stop. Put this book down and pick up *Simply Strategic Stuff: Help for Leaders Drowning in the Details of Running a Church* by Tim Stevens and Tony Morgan (available at group.com or wiredchurches.com). You'll find Chapters 8, 39, and 85 to be particularly helpful in determining your church's mission. I also recommend Rick Warren's *The Purpose-Driven Church* (available at purposedriven.com). A common mission unifies a congregation's focus and energizes ministry. People who do not gather around a shared mission will pursue multiple goals and directions. Distractions will abound. The absence of a common mission will generally result in disparate outcomes.

When your mission is clear, each ministry within your church must align with it. The objective of our guest services ministry comes from our central mission: "Helping people take their next step toward Christ...together." Our guest services mission is to "create an atmosphere of warmth and personal acceptance, providing a safe environment for people to take their next step toward Christ." This objective wasn't defined overnight. It was the product of prayer, conversation, and rewriting. It's now part of every training session we offer to new team members. We revisit it when we're all together. We've added it to our written communications to team members. These are constant reminders that we all want the same outcome.

Are your teams singing the same song for the same reason?

Your Guests: The "Who" of Your Mission

Once your mission is clear, you must determine who your mission will affect. While the immediate answer is "God's love is for everybody," your church will address people in your community that no other church will reach. In *The Purpose-Driven Church*, Rick Warren points to Jesus' identification of his focus: "I was sent only to the lost sheep of Israel" (Matthew 15:24). Warren adds, "Jesus targeted his ministry in order to be effective, not to be exclusive."[2]

When your focus is clear, you'll be able to effectively address your guests' needs. Identifying the people you will best reach, based on your church's makeup and your community's profile, will determine *how* you do ministry. For example, understanding the profile of your guests will affect how your teams dress and what kinds of greeting you offer. It will influence both the content and the style of your printed material. Based on your focus, you will develop your core values, your Sunday morning service, and your facility.

Knowing your church, your mission, and your focus will help you appropriately apply the ideas in this book. Anything you apply from this or any resource must be personalized to fit the culture and nature of *your* church.

Be you. Be true to what God has called you to be. When the people in your church know and share its Christ-focused mission, the gates of hell will not prevail against you! You've got Jesus' word on that (Matthew 16:18).

Can somebody say "Wow"?

Ask the Right People

When you understand the what and the who of your ministry, you'll know who can give you the best feedback about your guests' experiences. It's not the pastor or the church board. It's not even your greeter team. It's your guests. Ask your guests. They're the only ones who can give you feedback about their encounters.

Why do we forget that? Why would we rather rely on reports, statistics, and our own guesses about the guests in our churches? Marc Strachan, cofounder of Vigilante, a small but successful ad agency in Manhattan, says listening must precede talking. "It's hard to know what to say to someone when you don't understand what that person cares about."[3]

It's hard to know what to say to someone when you don't understand what that person cares about.

I've often thought that those of us in the church are among the poorest listeners. It's true we have a lot to talk about. I guess we figure we know God's message, and we just want to get it out there. But when we take the time to listen first, when we understand motivations, questions, and needs, we're better able to shape the delivery of our message. When we listen, we can understand. When we understand, we can enter conversation. Then, and only then, will our message be received.

The late leadership guru Stephen Covey identified listening as one of seven "highly effective" habits: "Seek first to understand, then to be understood."[4] It's about being interested, even empathic. It's about getting inside other people's worlds. It's not about judging or dismantling their worlds; it's about caring. Listening first is a key to grace-filled community.

Get Their Input Every Week

People love to be heard. They love to know that their input can be a catalyst to create a change that helps serve them. Have you ever completed a survey online? Why did you do that? McDonald's, Old Navy, Walmart, and Starbucks all ask for feedback through online surveys. They know that people appreciate it when their opinions are valued.

That's why we at Granger are intentional about getting feedback from our people every weekend. The service program (or bulletin) has a perforated "comment card" that we encourage guests to complete during the service. In addition to providing room for prayer concerns and ministry interests, it simply asks our guests to "Tell us about your experience." These comments have prompted us to recast vision, address needs in subsequent weekend messages, follow up personally, and celebrate that the message of Christ is intersecting the lives of our people.

Ask Them in a Survey

Periodically, we ask our entire church to participate in surveys that help us know how we're communicating, what needs exist, and how people are growing. We want their opinions about the music, the children's ministry, and guest services. We want to know about their ministry involvement. We ask them to help us evaluate our response time to inquiries and requests at the guest services center and the administrative office. We ask and we listen because people matter to us.

Hearing honest feedback is so important to us that at times we devote an entire weekend service to completing the survey. We shorten the time of the weekend message and put the focus on our vision and mission.

Rather than communicating how well we think we're doing with the mission and vision, we ask our people, including our newest guests, to give us their feedback. Sometimes the survey is a brief element in our service time. More often it is an online exercise.

A few months after the survey has been completed and compiled, we communicate the results. Generally the findings help us recast our vision because it is human to forget why we do what we do. Often the results help us refocus how we do ministry. We usually see strategies we need to alter to authentically communicate an ancient message in a relevant manner. We will keep asking.

Ask People Who Aren't Guests Yet

Several years ago, one of my staff members invited her friends who weren't attending church to visit our services and tell her about their experience. A month later, people who had never attended our church were on our campus to evaluate our weekend experience.

These "mystery shoppers" found our atmosphere warm and engaging, our team members approachable, and the overall experience excellent. But they also echoed a sentiment we'd begun to hear from other guests: We were a little "too friendly."

They helped us discover that the placement of our team members had created an intimidating, human wall. Our efforts to speak to as many of our guests as possible were perceived as overkill. More timid guests wanted to dodge and dart around the friendly greeters all the way through the lobby. Our layering of greeters had resulted in too many greetings and handshakes before guests reached the auditorium.

The "secret shopper" initiative was not sophisticated, costly, or burdensome. It required a little courage, but it was well worth the risk. I encourage you to try it. After all, people who don't attend your church will give the most honest feedback.

Just Ask

The best way to discover what your guests are experiencing is to simply ask them. You don't have to spend a lot of money to gain information you can't live without. Devise your own surveys. George Gallup Jr. and D. Michael

Lindsay offer hands-on survey tools in *The Gallup Guide: Reality Check for 21st Century Churches* (Group Publishing, 2002). This user-friendly book offers step-by-step checklists for developing your own questionnaires about any topic in any size of church. It even includes 10 reproducible surveys.

> **P**eople who don't attend your church will give the most honest feedback.

In addition, don't underestimate the power of response cards, informal conversations, and mystery shoppers.

Seek first to understand, then seek to be understood. If your guests are satisfied, they'll tell you. If they're dissatisfied, they'll tell you. Just ask.

Beyond Satisfaction to Engagement

Whatever your guests tell you about the care you're providing, there's more to serving than satisfying. When guests experience something more than satisfaction, they become engaged.

Benson Smith and Tony Rutigliano of the Gallup Organization address the difference between guest *satisfaction* and guest *engagement* in their book *Discover Your Sales Strengths* (Warner Books, 2003). While their work focuses on sales and customers, the results are directly transferable to your church, because their findings are rooted in human relationships. A guest can remain rather disconnected from the business or organization and be quite satisfied. Engaged guests have a *relationship* with the *people* who make up the organization. According to Smith and Rutigliano, up to 80 percent of customers claimed they were *satisfied*, while those who felt *engaged* amounted to only 40 percent or less.[5]

When guests and members of your church are engaged, there will be high levels of trust, respect, pride, and commitment. Consistency is a key quantifier when evaluating engagement. For instance, a guest cannot only trust certain people in your church and remain engaged; the trust must be thorough and consistent. To be truly engaged, one must feel consistently proud to be associated with your church. Engagement, then, is about healthy relationships.

If you want to see your guests engaged, rather than merely satisfied, you must define your mission clearly, listen to honest feedback, and remove potential distractions. It is much easier to merely satisfy your church's guests than to help them fully engage. But our calling is to help people take steps from consumer to connected, from connected to committed.

Try These Next Steps...

- What potential distractions are you aware of right now, without further investigation?

- Where will you visit within the next 30 days to assess the "Wows" in other settings and contrast them to your church?

- Who could help you better understand how guests might be distracted and how you might remove the hindrances?

- What steps will you take to listen to your guests about their experiences?

- How will you gauge trust levels among your members and guests?

Endnotes

1. Fred Crawford and Ryan Mathews, *The Myth of Excellence* (New York: Three Rivers Press, 2001) 164-165.

2. Rick Warren, *The Purpose-Driven Church* (Grand Rapids, MI: Zondervan Publishing House, 1995), 158.

3. Anna Muoio, "Beyond the City Limits," FastCompany (July 2000), 228.

4. Stephen Covey, *The Seven Habits of Highly Effective People* (New York: Simon & Schuster, 1989), 235.

5. Benson Smith and Tony Rutigliano, gallup.com, March 13, 2003.

Be the Guest

Use the following questions to record your experience when visiting a new place. This tool can be used in churches, restaurants, airports, malls, museums, and libraries. But don't stop there—any place you experience can be evaluated. Have fun!

- **Sight:** What do you see? What's distracting? What shows a lack of care or of excellence? Are signs well placed, helping you find your way around? How do shapes, colors, and images influence your experience? How does what you see affect your mood or state of mind?

_____

_____

_____

- **Smell:** Pay attention to odors. Are they pleasant? Do they help you relax, raise your curiosity, or make you hungry? Do you want to stay, or are you thinking, "I've got to get out of here"?

_____

_____

_____

- **Taste:** If you're dining, rate the quality of the food. If you're not dining, would food have been a good idea?

_____

_____

_____

■ **_Touch:_** Pay attention to textures. Are you invited to experience anything? How is your experience influenced by this sense? What would have enhanced your experience?

_____

_____

_____

■ **_Hearing:_** What do you hear? How did any intentional sounds as well as unplanned noises affect your experience? What would you have preferred to have heard?

_____

_____

_____

■ **_People:_** Were staff members appropriately personable and professional? Were they knowledgeable? Were they prepared?

_____

_____

_____

■ **_Other:_** Did you feel alienated in any way? What was confusing? What was designed with guests in mind? Note anything that was a distraction _or_ caused you to think "Wow!"

_____

_____

_____

3

Company's Coming. Are You Ready to Wow Them?

"Live wisely among those who are not Christians, and make the most of every opportunity."
(Colossians 4:5, New Living Translation)

Defining the Experience Before the Experience

I like using my GPS iPhone app because I get a turn-by-turn description of my path: "Turn right onto Johnson Road. 1.5 miles. Turn left onto U.S. 20. 4.5 miles." Before I leave the house, I have a map of the journey on my phone. I can see that I'm going to make a lot of turns and go through several small towns; best of all, I'll know when I get there. The same is true for whatever GPS device or service you use.

The late Stephen Covey's second habit of highly effective people is "Begin with the end in mind."[1] Before our guests arrive, we need to envision the experience we desire for them. If we can see that experience clearly, we can create a road map to lead them there.

What do you want people to feel? What emotions do you want them to experience within the first few minutes? What do you want them to see, touch, hear, and smell? It may help to put yourself in their shoes and ask what *they* want to feel. What do any of us want to feel in a new place?

I don't know about you, but when I go somewhere new, I want to feel special and valued. I want to feel free to be myself—not restricted by expectations I don't understand.

Awkwardness

I remember my first romantic dinner back in early high school. I'd never seen so many forks! How was I going to manage to use all those forks in a single meal? Of course, I could not let anyone, especially my date, know of my ignorance. So I kept talking, looking around at everyone else. I fixed my napkin on my lap one more time. I salted my salad. I took a drink of water. I fidgeted with my napkin again. I kept watching, hoping someone at my table would pick up a fork and begin to eat soon.

As I looked around the table, I knew whom I could trust to follow. I don't know how I knew that; we'd never talked about forks before. I just knew she would know which fork to use first. I followed her lead and enjoyed the rest of the meal.

Can you remember a time you felt intimidated, awkward, and unsure of yourself? These feelings lead to a sense of alienation. This is definitely *not* what you want your guests to experience!

But if you fail to begin with the end in mind, that is exactly what will happen. Your guests may not feel comfortable in their chosen attire. They may not know where to go or when to sit or stand in your service. If they feel they failed to meet expectations for their behavior, they may never return.

Anticipating Your Guests' Experience

How do you want your guests to feel? List two or three emotions you'd like your guests to experience—not during the service but within their first few minutes on your campus.

_____

_____

_____

_____

Your church doesn't have to be large for your guests to feel this awkwardness. Any church can have its own "family traditions" that may unintentionally alienate guests. Do your guests know that refreshments are available in the fellowship hall? Are they welcome to participate? Are beverages allowed in your auditorium or sanctuary? Is a particular dress code communicated to new people? If you serve the Lord's Supper, do you assume everyone knows what to do?

Plan for Spontaneity

Sporting events, live concerts, zoos, and other interactive venues are designed to give rise to "planned spontaneity." Tremendous planning goes into parking, ticketing, traffic flow, concessions, and programming. But within those settings, spontaneity is what makes the events *memorable*. Who could forget catching a fly ball at a professional baseball game or watching a goat in a zoo's petting farm eat a little girl's hair ribbon? The challenge is to create an environment that allows spontaneous happenings consistent with your desired outcome.

> The challenge is to create an environment that allows spontaneous happenings consistent with your desired outcome.

Walt Disney envisioned what a guest's photo album might look like after the family vacation. Then the imagining began. Before the gates opened for the first time, he asked, "What do we want our guests to experience? What environments will we develop to encourage spontaneous moments?"

You certainly don't have total control over your guests' responses to the environment you create in your church. You can't control what relational connections they make. But you can create an environment, even multiple environments, that lead to the spontaneous responses you desire. Start by asking, "What potential do we want to create?"

A prayerfully, carefully planned environment can be an incubator for the work of the Holy Spirit. I think that's the reality inside spontaneous happenings in the church: They're God moments. When the right touch, a caring word, and a genuine exchange occur, people experience the love of Jesus!

> A prayerfully, carefully planned environment can be an incubator for the work of the Holy Spirit.

Anatomy of a Great Experience

When you can articulate what you want your guests to feel, or not feel; what you want them to see, or not see; what you want them to hear, or not hear; you've begun to build a great experience. Ask yourself, "What would I like to hear our guests saying at work on Monday about their visit to our church?" The answer to this question will clarify the outcome you want for your guests.

As we answered this question at Granger, we knew we wanted our guests to talk about how comfortable they felt. We knew that to accomplish this, we would have to depend, first and foremost, on people. People are the most important factor in determining the quality of your guests' experiences.

At Granger, we want to encourage interaction that helps people feel as comfortable as they might with their family or friends at the local mall. We've found that few things help people feel more comfortable in a new place than having a beverage in their hand, so our guests enter the building and walk right into a café area where they can get a cup of coffee or a soft drink. It's a simple social custom that creates a sense of normalcy. People feel more relaxed, even a bit in control of their experience, when they're holding a beverage. While we don't expect every guest to purchase coffee, our restaurant, The Eatery, offers a *normal* activity for guests to experience with others.

As you begin to picture the experience you desire for your guests, I encourage you to include others in your conversation. And I encourage you to review this picture every four to six months. It will change often.

Developing the Defined Experience...Slowly

I hope your dream is bigger than what you can pull off right now. That means you're truly dreaming; you're looking beyond where you are right now. And that's good, as long as you keep today in perspective. Don't become discouraged if you aren't where you want to be.

We didn't always have a café or restaurant. We didn't always have a well-placed guest services center. We've had to dream, develop, and design just like any other church or organization. Our church met in a theater for 10 years. Small tables and the concession stand served as the coffee bar and information center. It all came out of boxes every Sunday for a decade.

When we moved to our current campus in 1996, the gathering space for services was our atrium. We packed over 400 people into space for 327 each service—up to six times a weekend. We barely had room for a small information table at the farthest corner from the entrance, and we didn't serve coffee.

In the spring of 2000, we grew into the auditorium adjacent to the atrium space we had been using. For nearly four months during our expansion project, we lost the "farthest corner"—our information center. So we rented a small trailer, put it on the front lawn, and plastered the side of it with a banner reading "Dog-Ugly Resource Trailer." It was ugly, but people could find it.

Here's my point: Start where you are. The "if we can't do it all now we might as well not start" notion will cheat your guests, and it will rob your people of the opportunity to serve while creating the future of your ministry together.

You don't have to spend lots of money to create a "Wow!" experience. For instance, one of the simplest things we've done is to offer umbrella escorts from the curb across to the door of our building on rainy days. We invested only a few dollars, but the payoff has been huge. Start small, where you are, with what you have.

The "First 10 Minutes" Principle

Here's how seriously we've taken this challenge to define our guests' experience in advance. If our guests can't say, "Wow! I'm impressed!" within their first 10 minutes on campus, then we've failed.

Somewhere between the parking lot and the children's center, the 10 minutes pass. Somewhere between the restroom and the children's center, a typical parent or couple with children should be thinking, "Wow! I'm impressed!" That's our standard at Granger. Before the music starts, before the message is delivered, guests should be grateful to be present at Granger Community Church. They should know they matter to *us* before they hear how much they matter to *God*.

Jeffrey Gitomer says you can tell in a number of ways if you're accomplishing this. It may come in the form of direct feedback—you might actually hear someone say "Wow!" It may be in the form of a simple smile generated by exemplary service. Other times you may hear, "I can't thank you enough."[2] You may realize it when a guest returns to your church for the second or third week in a row. Or others may attend because of the report they heard at work on Monday morning from a friend who was wowed.

What could the "first 10 minutes" principle look like in your setting? What would a "Wow!" look like in your guest services ministry? Do you need to brew tea and bake crumpets to solicit a "Wow"? Do you need to offer "tipless" valet parking? Creating the "Wow!" experience in your church is all about *your* environment, *your* community, *your* guests, and how you'll best communicate that they matter to *you*.

If you currently have no organized greeter ministry, the creation of such a team could be a "Wow!" If you have greeters, but no one helping to park cars, you could begin to wow your guests with a traffic team. Maybe you have full guest services teams, but the "Wow!" will come when they actually arrive before your guests do. (It's a pretty significant step!)

You have just 10 minutes. In that time, will your guests say, "Wow! I'm impressed"?

Redefining "Wow!"

Of course, what's a "Wow!" today may not be a "Wow!" tomorrow. If a "Wow!" is done well, it will eventually become expected. It will become part of your desired reputation. But it will no longer be a "Wow!"

To be a "Wow!" an experience must be unexpected. The fresh-baked cookie at the DoubleTree, the bed at the Westin that feels better than your bed at home, and the free dessert on your birthday at your local grill are unexpected treats *the first time*. But over time, these experiences become the norm. To continue to wow their guests, these companies will have to create other surprising gestures of welcome.

Several years ago we created a new "Wow!" for our weekend guests. As the parking lot had grown to accommodate the weekend crowds, our guests were having to walk farther from their cars to the building. We watched these guests (new people in a new place for the first time) walk through the front doors of our church. In the winter they were shivering from their walk, focused on one thing: getting warm.

So in 2001 we received money through our Christmas offering to procure two 17-passenger vans to shuttle our guests from their cars to the building. The vans featured television monitors playing short videos highlighting our ministries. The seating was U-shaped, rather than in rows, to encourage community and openness. The drivers were part of our guest services team and were trained to provide safe, warm, dry transit to and from the building. That was *one* of our "Wow!" expressions. But over time—a decade—the shuttle required more budget for maintenance or replacement, and their usage became "tired," so we retired them.

Today, what was once a small café is a seven-day-per-week restaurant with soft seating and dining areas for guests to engage in conversation—on the weekends and throughout the week.

I'm still dreaming with other team members about the future at Granger. What might we offer some day that we aren't offering right now? How do we continually re-create the "Wow"?

I'm dreaming about the day we'll offer self-serve, touch-screen kiosks in the atrium lobby. Some guests would appreciate remaining somewhat anonymous while taking a next step. What if our guests could walk up to a free-standing touch screen with options that would allow them to access and print maps of the building or register for an event, retreat, group, or class?

"Wow!" is about innovation, and innovation is about addressing a constantly changing culture. We must be astute observers, conversationalists, and purveyors of change. Where will the next "Wow!" come from? Who will it come from?

Creating "Wows" Right Where You Are

Using the chart below, brainstorm potential "Wow!" scenarios alone or with a group. Starting with the left column, list 10 or more expectations of your guests. Then for each of those, use the center column to record what could possibly go wrong with that "normal expectation." That is, if a normal expectation is tissue in the restroom, a "potential negative experience" might be no tissue. Finally, in the right column record what could be done to enhance the normal expectation to create a "Wow!"

Normal Expectation	Potential Negative Experience	Potential "Wow!"

Look for the "Wow-Makers" Around You

Behind the warm cookie at the DoubleTree was a motive to wow guests. The heavenly bed at the Westin was probably a response to hundreds of complaints about uncomfortable hotel beds. Behind the shuttles at Granger was a vision to care. And behind every one of these ideas are people. "Wow!" experiences don't happen without wow-makers.

You may be a wow-maker, but you don't have to personally come up with every new and great idea. The strength of leadership isn't in creating every fresh idea; it is in recognizing and implementing the ideas of other wow-makers.

> **Wow-makers often start sentences by saying, "What if...?"**

Wow-makers are simply people who offer fresh ideas, new behaviors, or innovative solutions that cause guests to say "Wow!" And they are in your church. They're thinking now about how to make it better.

Wow-makers often start sentences by saying, "What if...?" Then they dream out loud, painting a picture of what could be. Wow-makers may offer their ideas in a focused brainstorming session, but more often they make suggestions on the fly as they watch guests and think about how their experiences could be enhanced.

Create ways for people to tell you their ideas. A simple box labeled "Wow-Making Ideas" could produce dozens of good suggestions. Listen to your team members as they serve beside you. Ask them how the team could better serve your guests. Set up an e-mail account specifically for innovative ideas. Offer prizes for creative ideas, whether or not they are used.

Granger's Guest Services Teams

As Granger has evolved, so have the scope and number of our guest services teams. Here is a description of the teams and their responsibilities. Your guest services ministry will reflect your church's unique culture and circumstances.

- **Traffic Team**—These teams, made up of men and women, serve in snow, rain, and sunshine, orchestrating the large number of cars coming in and out of the parking lots and helping guests find open parking spaces.

- **Usher/Greeter Team**—These teams serve in a six-week rotation, usually for the entire slate of weekend services. They greet guests at the curb, at the front doors, and at the entry to the auditorium. Inside the auditorium, ushers distribute bulletins, help guests find seats, and collect the offerings. At Granger, 30 ushers/greeters are needed for each service.

- **Guest Services Center Team**—This team answers questions, receives registrations, and handles phone inquiries during every service. These resourceful team members are detail-oriented, have strong organizational skills, and are able to handle money competently.

- **Campus Guides**—These team members provide personal attention to new guests, escorting families with young children to the children's center, answering questions, and orienting guests to our church.

- **Reads & Things**—This staff of volunteers encourages leisurely browsing, offering assistance to new guests and regular attendees as they select various resources for spiritual growth.

- **The Eatery Restaurant/Café**—This team helps create a welcoming atmosphere, encouraging connectivity and conversation over a cup of coffee.

- **Bulletin Assembly Team**—This behind-the-scenes team comes in on Saturday afternoons to assemble thousands of bulletins for the weekend services.

- **"White Glove" Housekeeping Team**—These individuals keep the glass sparkling, the sinks clean, and the restroom tissue stocked. They keep the facility in a condition of newness, thereby removing potential distractions from our guests' experiences on campus.

- **Safety Team**—These weekend volunteers are trained professionals who work in the community with various police departments. Their presence provides a sense of security.

- **Medical Response Team**—These team members wear vibrating beepers during the service of their preference. Up to four team members are present for each service. They are trained in CPR and defibrillator and supplemental oxygen use.

- **Point Person**—These folks serve as communication leaders during all public gatherings. They supervise radio communication as well as emergency plans for the entire campus. They function independently and work on rotating weekends.

The "Wow!" SHAPE: Fit Matters

For a long time around Granger, people would quip, "If you can brush your teeth and smile, you can serve on a guest services team." It's just not so. These team members need more than fresh breath and a nice smile. They need to know how to connect with people, and they need to enjoy doing so. They should be wow-makers. How God has designed individuals determines where and how they should serve in the local church. Not every member of your church should be a member of your guest services team.

This deserves some attention: Who should make up the guest services team? Who are these ushers? What's the makeup of a greeter? How should a guest services team member be wired?

"The old adage 'People are your most important asset' turns out to be wrong. People are not your most important asset. The right people are."[3]
—Jim Collins

Around Granger we've adopted an effective acronym penned by Saddleback Church's senior pastor, Rick Warren. To help people understand and discover their unique wiring, Rick uses this five-point acronym: SHAPE (**S**piritual Gifts, **H**eart, **A**bilities, **P**ersonality, and **E**xperiences). Let's examine these elements further.

"So since we find ourselves fashioned into all these excellently formed and marvelously functioning parts in Christ's body, let's just go ahead and be what we were made to be."
(Romans 12:5, The Message)

Spiritual Gifts

Spiritual gifts are divine enablements given by the Holy Spirit to equip each believer for significance and purpose and to be a witness of God's grace to the world. Gifts such as hospitality and encouragement can be invaluable ministry assets on a first impressions team. Certainly other gifts may also be represented on these teams. For example, the gifts of administration and leadership are certainly essential for those leading and overseeing the ministry of these teams. Rick Warren puts it this way in

The Purpose-Driven Life: "When we use our gifts together, we all benefit. If others don't use their gifts, you get cheated, and if you don't use your gifts, they get cheated."[4] The ministry of first impressions will bear fruit as people exercise their spiritual gifts.

Heart

The H in the acronym is for *heart*; that is, passion. Every person has a fondness for a certain cause, need, or group of people. This is reflected in our conversations and is deeply tied to our emotions. While some adults may have difficulty unearthing it, a personal passion is buried somewhere in each of us.

Sometimes passion is manifested in the form of criticism. What may initially sound like a complaint may actually reflect a desire to make a difference! People may tend to see all the problems in an area about which they're passionate, and that may be all you hear from them. If we dismiss these people as whiners and troublemakers, we may overlook key players who are driven by their passions.

On the other hand, some people really are chronic complainers. If that's the case, direct them toward appropriate help. They need to be ministered *to*; they shouldn't be leading others.

Pay attention to passion. Every member on your team should be passionate about relating to and connecting with people.

Abilities

There are dozens of skill sets that contribute to the components of a first impressions ministry. Listening, communicating, question-asking, counting, guiding, directing, perceiving, and disseminating are all helpful abilities. The key is to help people identify their many skills and use them fully as they minister. When your people are encouraged to engage as many of their abilities and gifts as possible, they will experience tremendous fulfillment.

Personality

When someone steps up to serve on a greeter team, it's easy to say, "Great! Come join us!" The volunteer's personality, however, is critical in helping you and the volunteer understand how he or she is wired to serve.

At Granger, an introverted, quiet person who is passionate that people feel welcome may be comfortable serving on some teams but not on others. For instance, we wouldn't ask this person to serve at the guest services center; we may, however, ask him or her to serve on the bulletin-assembly team. For those who are greeting people face to face, an extroverted personality is a must.

Experiences

Work experience, former church ministry experience, and painful experiences all contribute to the way people define their roles. Former or current employment—especially in sales and other areas of customer service—may help a team member excel at honoring God and wowing your guests. Every experience counts. God wastes nothing.

As you define the *experience* you want your guests to have, you simultaneously define the *team member* to help create that experience. Tapping people in your church with the "Wow!" SHAPE will bring rich fulfillment to them, and your guests will feel welcome and at home.

Recognize that everyone is unique, and celebrate that individuality. When you help each person find the right place in which to serve, everyone wins.

Finding the Right Fit for Guest Services

The following table suggests spiritual gifts, personality traits, and abilities helpful in fulfilling each of the guest services roles we've identified at Granger. Use all or part of the chart to help you build profiles and then recruit and review team members.

> As you define the experience you want your guests to have, you simultaneously define the team member to help create that experience.

Ministry Role	Spiritual Gifts	Personality	Abilities
Traffic coordinator	Administration or helps	Any	Follows directions well, is calm and cordial under pressure
Greeter	Hospitality or encouragement	Extroverted	Makes people feel welcome without smothering them

Ministry Role	Spiritual Gifts	Personality	Abilities
Guest services information center specialist	Hospitality or administration	Extroverted	Is detail-oriented, a public relations expert, has broad knowledge of the church network and ministries
Campus guide	Hospitality or encouragement	Extroverted	Has knowledge of the building and ministries, is professional and personable
Usher	Hospitality or encouragement	Extroverted	Is calm and cordial under pressure, discreet, sensitive
Restaurant/ bookstore attendant	Hospitality, helps, or administration	Extroverted	Is organized, detail-oriented, loves the product as well as people
Bulletin assembler	Helps	Introverted	Is organized, works at a fast pace
White-glove attendant	Helps	Any	Is detail-oriented, flexible
Safety specialist	Administration or leadership	Any	Is detail-oriented, observant, calm under pressure, has security training
Medical responder	Helps	Any	Has CPR training, is calm under pressure
Point person	Leadership or administration	Extroverted	Is highly organized and detail-oriented, has broad interpersonal skills

"Wow" People Attract "Wow-Makers"

In his book *The 21 Irrefutable Laws of Leadership*, John Maxwell describes the "Law of Magnetism: Who you are is who you attract."[5] As you build your teams according to their members' SHAPEs, pay attention to this law, especially as it applies to leadership.

Several years ago, I managed a retail clothing store. My regional manager told me that if I would build a strong team with a strong sense of belonging and fun, I would never have difficulty recruiting new team members. As I cast this vision to individuals, people began to join the team. During that first year, my assistant, Alan, and I built a team that felt as if it were a family. The sense of fun in the store was contagious. Mall walkers would stop by just to talk, and repeat customers visited the store, even when they weren't buying. We had created a "Wow!" culture that cut recruiting efforts in half; people wanted to be part of a fun and welcoming environment!

As you build your leadership team, paint the picture of the kind of experience you're trying to create for your guests. Describe the eternal merits of this ministry. As they hear a compelling, "gotta be a part of that" vision, they'll step up to be part of something bigger than themselves, and they'll pass that vision along to their teams.

"A carefully crafted vision has the ability to capture people's imaginations as well as their commitment. People will reprioritize their lives and lifestyles in order to be a part of a vision they feel called to."[6]
—Andy Stanley

Remember, your core leadership team will determine what the rest of your team looks like. When you build a team of wow-makers, they will attract other wow-makers. Excellence attracts excellence; fun generates fun.

Our guest services teams are as good as they are because of their leaders. Honor the law of magnetism, and it will honor you.

"Wow!" people create "Wow!" experiences. Company's coming. Get ready to wow them!

Try These Next Steps...

- Dream the dream. What would you like to hear your guests saying on Monday morning at their workplaces about their experience at your church?

- What steps will you take to define this preferred experience for your guests?

- What "adequate" moment could you turn into a "Wow!" moment within the next 30 days? Can you think of two or three over the next quarter?

- How will you apply the SHAPE strategy to your team-building efforts?

- In the upcoming week, what potential leaders will you speak with regarding your vision?

Endnotes

1. Stephen Covey, *The Seven Habits of Highly Effective People* (New York: Simon & Schuster, 1989), 95.

2. Jeffrey Gitomer, *Customer Satisfaction Is Worthless, Customer Loyalty Is Priceless* (Atlanta: Bard Press, 1998), 98.

3. Jim Collins, *Good to Great* (New York: HarperCollins Publishers, Inc., 2001),13.

4. Rick Warren, *The Purpose-Driven Life* (Grand Rapids, MI: Zondervan, 2002), 237.

5. John Maxwell, *The 21 Irrefutable Laws of Leadership* (Nashville, TN: Thomas Nelson, Inc., 1998), 89.

6. Andy Stanley, *Visioneering* (Sisters, OR: Multnomah Publishers, Inc, 1999), 106.

4

Creating the "Wow!" Experience From the Outside In

"Here is a simple, rule-of-thumb guide for behavior: Ask yourself what you want people to do for you, then grab the initiative and do it for them." (Matthew 7:12, The Message)

Senior Leadership Support: Don't Start Without It

So where do you start, especially if you've not really gotten a guest services ministry officially off the ground? You'll need to start with your senior leadership. And if you've started without it, I urge you to revisit this crucial step. Chances are, you've experienced some difficulty without it.

At a recent conference—presented annually on our campus by our ministry to church ministries across the country (visit wiredchurches.com for more information)—I heard our senior pastor, Mark Beeson, say, "Pastors, the stuff that happens outside the auditorium is every bit as important as the stuff that happens inside the auditorium." Our executive pastor, Tim Stevens, added: "The strength of your first impressions ministries… directly correlates to the value your senior leadership places on those areas. It is vital your senior team has agreement and consensus and alignment on the mission, vision, and values. This drives everything. It affects budgets, staffing, resources, and priorities. Before you change your activity, you must change your philosophy. You must have agreement at the top about how important your various ministries are."

Before you change your activity, you must change your philosophy.

You may be fired up. Other people may be fired up. But unless you have the support of the senior leadership in your church, you'll never get the fire to take hold. If you're not the senior pastor, schedule time with him or her to talk about your dream for your church's ministry to newcomers. Buy a copy of this book for your senior pastor, and ask for time to discuss it.

During your discussions, address the following questions thoroughly so you can clearly communicate the vision of your new ministry as it develops.

1. What is your mission? What defines your church? How will you know when your church is successful?

2. What specific group of people are you trying to reach with the good news of Christ?

3. What experience do you want for your guests on campus? How would you define it in advance? What would you want them to talk about on Monday morning at their workplace?

4. What is the layout of your campus and church buildings? What is the current traffic flow for cars in the parking lot and people in the building? How could this be improved, allowing guests easier entries and exits?

Form or Function: Which Comes First?

You may have noticed that within these four sets of questions are two primary factors: people and buildings. As you're making decisions about people and team development—what kinds of teams, who makes up those teams, who leads those teams—it's important to remember that the *function* you want your guest services teams to render will determine the *form* your structure takes. (We'll discuss this more thoroughly in following chapters.)

Function, by necessity, will follow the *form* of your physical structure.

However, when it comes to buildings, the opposite is true. *Function*, by necessity, will follow the *form* of your physical structure. So you want to build knowing your facility will either limit or enhance the function of your ministry. Whether you own, rent, borrow, or are constructing your building, you'll want to pay attention to how it affects your guest services ministry (more on this in Chapter 5).

On a sheet of graph paper, plot your campus footprint (no one will be checking for artistic ability). Include the parking lot and buildings. Indicate all entry points—both to your parking areas and to your buildings. These may suggest points at which you'll place team members to greet or assist your guests.

Monitor Your Peak Traffic Times

Next, note traffic flow. What are the peak times in the parking lot? When do the largest crowds come through your front doors? What special needs might this suggest? Have you ever shopped in a store that was understaffed during the height of the Christmas season? Its staffing was probably adequate on a Monday morning in mid-March, but the staffing need is much greater on the day after Thanksgiving!

I remember when Krispy Kreme Doughnuts opened in our town. For 22 days I had watched the billboard-sized countdown to grand opening day. I was so pumped! If you've been to Krispy Kreme, you know that the time to buy their doughnuts is when the neon-red "hot" sign is glowing. This indicates the doughnuts are coming off the conveyor line—piping hot, freshly glazed in a bath of sugar, and ready for mouth-watering consumption. It's doughnut heaven!

Opening day came. Twelve cars were lined up in the drive-through lane. The parking lot was full of customers' cars and media vans. I managed to find a place to park as another customer pulled out, doughnut in hand. I was prepared to wait in line for a while, knowing it was opening day and the store was filled to capacity. Much to my surprise, however, I walked up to the counter (after receiving a free doughnut from the greeter at the front door), ordered two dozen original glazed, and paid for them. I was in and out of the store in less than two minutes.

Krispy Kreme scheduled for peak traffic.

Every once in a while, I purposely come to church during the busiest service on Sunday morning. I want to experience the wait time for myself, the demeanor of our hired police officers, and the efficiency of our traffic teams. Once I'm headed to the building, I experience the friendliness of our greeters and hospitality team members. I observe the line of parents waiting to check their children into their classrooms. This is one of the best ways for me to evaluate how we're doing during peak times.

Keep your answers to the four questions on page 56 and your graph paper nearby. Over the next few pages, we'll explore these questions, and more, as you visualize your guests' experience from the time they arrive at your campus until the time they leave.

Stuck in Traffic

There are some things you can't change, at least not in the near future. The traffic flow in front of your main entrance is one example. Unless you happen to have a traffic light at your parking lot entrance, there's probably little you can do to direct traffic on the road. What can you do when your guests can't easily get in and out of your parking lot?

Your Evaluation: Are your guests waiting in their cars on the street to turn into your property? Does oncoming traffic prevent them from moving safely and quickly out of your parking lot? If your church offers multiple services, are you experiencing gridlock in the parking lot between services?

Here's the reality about many of your guests. They don't yet share the same values that bring Christ-followers to your campus. They're still kicking the tires; they're checking out the claims of Christ. They don't feel the need, the innate desire, or the obligation to return to your services. It's your job to make that experience as painless, hassle free, and extraordinary as possible. Otherwise, the 5-minute wait to get into your parking lot or the 20-minute wait to leave may be a real impediment to their return.

Granger's Model: Several years ago, we began to experience this very thing. Guests were lined up 12 to 15 cars deep on the street, trying to get into our parking lot. Recent retail development in the area had turned this street into a major thoroughfare, preventing cars from turning left into the lot. In addition, the same traffic made it difficult to leave when the service was over. All of this was true in spite of a fairly new rear entrance to the north.

Ultimately, we chose to budget and hire off-duty city police officers to assist guests during peak hours on Sunday mornings. This protects our team members and the church from unnecessary liability issues, while helping guests see that they matter enough for us to increase traffic efficiency at entrances and exits.

Every few months we conduct an analysis to weigh the value of our partnership with our city police. Are we scheduling their service at the right time? Are our parking teams properly staffed to coordinate well with their efforts?

Not Even Out of the Car Yet: Irritated or Impressed?

For years the entrance to the parking lot of our local mall was a model of inefficiency. This entrance, off the busiest street in the area, ran into a mall intersection within one small-car length from the road. Cars pulling into the parking area off the busy street weren't supposed to stop, but they *always* did! If you were in the second car attempting to use the entrance from Grape Road, you were likely to get hit by oncoming traffic. Many mall shoppers were angered every day by the poor traffic flow into the parking lot. It was a ridiculous setup.

It *was.* An investment in a major construction project now winds entering traffic more deeply into the mall property, sparing anxiety and avoiding accidents.

Your Evaluation: What do your guests experience as they enter your church's parking lot? Are parking spaces easy to locate and access? Are core members and regular attendees parking away from the building, creating premium space for guests near the entrance to the building? Would traffic flow and ease of parking be improved if teams were available to direct cars?

I once visited a church that had taken proactive steps to provide spaces near the building. Rather than "Reserved for Pastor" signs near a main entrance, the church had posted signs that read "Guest Parking." That's more like it! Then I counted. There were only five signs. This was a church of over 300, but there were only five parking spaces reserved for guests. I wondered if they expected only five or fewer guests at any one service. At least it was a step in the right direction.

Recently I've visited churches with an average attendance of about 200 people on the weekend. At first glance their parking lots don't seem to necessitate large traffic teams. But I wonder about peak times before and after services. What if each of these churches provided even one or two people to direct cars to open spaces? How would this simple change improve guests' experiences within their first few seconds on the property?

Granger's Model: As I've mentioned previously, we manage our parking areas with trained, unpaid traffic teams whose role is to help guests find parking places quickly and efficiently. They serve during peak times. At one time these teams served only on Sunday mornings, until our Saturday evening services created enough volume to warrant their help. They are equipped with standard traffic-control gear such as fluorescent vests, flashlight wands, and radios for team communication.

Other "Wow!" Models: On a visit to Saddleback Church some time ago, I experienced the "Wow!" of their parking attendants. As some friends and I neared the main parking area on Saddleback's campus, signs directed us to a special "visitor parking" area to the left of other cars that were already parked. Vested, light-shining traffic attendants directed us to an empty space, where we were met by a greeter who opened our car doors and heartily welcomed us. We were then welcomed several more times as we made our way to the building. I appreciated the initiative this ministry team had taken to identify and welcome its guests. However, keep in mind that not every new guest wants the attention that comes with special parking. Don't force the guest parking.

Another church team I know washes the windows of guests' cars during services. Another church offers valet parking—without charge—to guests who desire it.

Your Opportunity: What will you do to create an experience that causes your guests to exclaim "Wow!" before they ever get to your building? The answer to that question will depend on your community and the culture of your local ministry.

At Granger we don't open car doors for guests in the parking lot (except to help single parents and the elderly at the curb drop-off); it doesn't fit our culture. We haven't started washing windows yet—we're not sure the risk of multiple alarms being set off during the service is worth the "Wow!" potential. We may not take on the liability that is inherent with valet parking.

But you're not Granger. Large or small, many or few—find a way to create a "Wow!" experience in your parking lot before your guests ever head to the building.

Make the Walk to the Building as Short as Possible

You can't control the weather, but it sure can affect your guests' experience on your campus. How you respond to the elements is critical to your guests' encounter with your church.

Your Evaluation: Who clears the snow from your parking lot in the winter? Does ice build up in certain spots that might cause a guest to fall? What might you do to keep your guests dry as they move from their cars to the building when it's raining? Is anyone available to help single parents with young children? Who is at the drop-off area to assist the elderly? What are you doing now that creates a positive buzz among your guests? What could you do that might produce a "Wow!" once each car is parked?

Granger's Model: Our greeter teams typically provide at least one person at the curb of the main entrance to acknowledge people with a warm hello or smile. These greeters are available to open car doors for people being dropped off by their drivers. We have some team members who actually insist on serving at the curb, regardless of the weather! This role carries no expense, and it rates high on the "Wow!" meter for many of our guests.

> You can't control the weather, but it sure can affect your guests' experience on your campus.

Additional greeters use umbrellas to help people into the building on rainy days. Again, the investment is minimal but the yield is remarkable!

Other "Wow!" Models: One summer on vacation my family and I enjoyed an evening meal at a seafood restaurant in Atlanta. Although the rain was light as we headed inside, we were immediately grateful for a long canopy extending from the front door to the lower part of the parking lot where we parked. This was another example of a low-expense, high-return investment in guest satisfaction. We entered the dining area that evening dry, comfortable, and impressed.

Your Opportunity: I encourage you to keep it simple. You don't have to spend money you don't have. You could ask members to donate umbrellas. Members' minivans or SUVs could be used to provide rides to the building. Placing someone at the curb to help single parents with children makes a lot of sense and costs nothing.

Invest what you do have to create the defined experience. Maybe you could buy uniform umbrellas and add your church name or logo. Perhaps you could invest in golf carts for the ride to the building. What about constructing an awning from your door to the parking lot?

Where will you create the "Wow!" for your guests *before* they enter your church building?

Greeters—at Every Entry Point

Back in my retail days, other sales associates and I used to enter the mall through back entrances before and after hours. My family and I used these entrances too because they were between main entrances and, therefore, near open parking spaces. We often use side entrances to larger "super" stores to avoid crowded entries.

Your Evaluation: Does your church have entries other than the main entrance? Who uses those access points? Are they reserved only for staff and lay leaders, or could guests also enter your building through those doors?

Granger's Model: As our building has expanded, we have increased the points of entry. Although most people use our new main entrances, some of them continue to utilize a smaller lower-level entrance, accessed from our lower parking area, with access to our children's center. When guests enter there, we want them to experience the same warm greeting that the crowd upstairs does. So we assign greeters there, too. At every door, people are positioned to say "Welcome!" Their role is to open the door for guests and greet them cordially.

As guests walk toward the entrance, we want them to see people with whom they identify. We want them to look around and realize, "They're like me. I'll be OK here. I fit." Even if that thought is not a conscious one, we want to eliminate any feeling of not belonging. So attention is given to age, gender, and personality as we decide from week to week who will be serving at the exterior entry points. If every person serving along the front of the church is under the age of 25, a 52-year-old couple may not readily see people like themselves. Or if six 55-year-olds line the front, our 21-year-old guest may feel equally out of place. Our teams represent a broad spectrum of our weekend crowd; we are intentional about representing diversity in gender and stage of life on each team. Students to seniors, males and females, greet our guests each week.

Other "Wow!" Models: At varying extremes on the fashion scale, both Walmart and stores along Rodeo Drive greet their customers at the front door. A growing number of restaurants are greeting patrons at the door, welcoming them and sometimes taking dining party information to expedite the wait inside.

Dave and Buster's, a restaurant and arcade wonderland, makes a statement through their door greeters that made an indelible impression on my wife. When I asked her what establishment has made a positive initial impression on her, she recalled our evening at Dave and Buster's. Dressed to the nines—black suit, tie, the works—the doormen announce with their presence, attire, and cordial demeanor that an experience of personal, professional attention awaits inside.

Your Opportunity: What will you do to welcome your guests to an extraordinary experience? Inside your doors they will hear of the love of Christ. They will be invited to engage in life-changing relationships, particularly with a God who invites them to come "home." What will you do to lay out the welcome mat as they enter your doors?

They will be invited to engage in life-changing relationships, particularly with a God who invites them to come "home." What will you do to lay out the welcome mat as they enter your doors?

To Shake or Not to Shake: That Is the Question

There are two extremes I've noticed when it comes to greeters. These two extremes can be labeled as "hands-off" and "hands-on." Let me explain.

For years Willow Creek Community Church in South Barrington, Illinois, practiced a philosophy of ministry that appropriately showed up in their weekend approach to greeting. Willow wanted to provide an opportunity for the unchurched to explore Jesus and his claims at their own pace. They didn't want to present themselves as pushy, dogmatic, or self-righteous. They developed a culture of "check it out" that was safe.

In those days, guests would walk into Willow's building the same way they would walk into their neighborhood mall. No greeters at all. Once inside, there were people who appeared available near or behind information centers, but a guest might not be overtly offered a handshake.

There was no mistake in this. No one was dropping the ball. This was all by design. They offered personal space to their guests, providing visible help if it was desired, but they did not approach with an "eye-to-eye" handshake. Guests were made to feel comfortable and safe.

At the same time on the other side of the country, Saddleback Church in Lake Forest, California, was declaring "Welcome home to your family!" with every greeting. Guests would receive a robust handshake, maybe a hearty pat on the shoulder, and an enthusiastic welcome. Saddleback's philosophy was to include, involve, and embrace every person as soon as possible. They wanted every guest to not only feel welcome but at home.

Today, Willow's philosophy has changed. While guests are not likely to experience the over-the-top embrace they'd receive at Saddleback still today, Willow Creek is intentional to greet and engage their guests. They've changed because the culture has shifted. For the most part, people want to be acknowledged. Even at church. They show up for help and hope and trust that caring people will be part of that experience.

At Granger we've worked over the years at understanding our guests and their expectations. We've learned from surveys and comments that when people come to our church they want to engage genuine people who help them feel comfortable, even safe. That can mean a number of different things to people. Do they want a handshake? Do they want to be touched at all?

We've decided to let them tell us! No, we don't ask people, "May I shake your hand?" If we did, many people would shove their hands deeply into their pockets and walk away! Instead, we let them tell us by their body language how they prefer to be greeted.

> We are committed to helping our guests experience a warm, inviting atmosphere, helping them feel safe and open to what's next.

Are their hands in their pockets; are they averting their eyes; is their pace hurried? In this case, is it rude not to offer a handshake? No, all of these gestures suggest to us that these guests do not want a handshake. Above all, we want to respect their wishes.

We are committed to helping our guests experience a warm, inviting atmosphere, helping them feel safe and open to what's next. So we try to be congenial, as well as sensitive, as we show respect to and personally acknowledge our guests.

How we practice congeniality with sensitivity is constantly challenged. Several years ago when we added a second Saturday evening service, we intentionally targeted a more youthful crowd (wanna-be-younger-than-I-really-am types like me showed up, too) for a later, 7:30 p.m. service. Within weeks we realized that there was a profoundly different set of general expectations for interaction with this crowd.

We asked all our guest services teams to ratchet it down a bit. Forgo the handshake. Open fewer car doors. Don't necessarily stand on the curb. Feel free to drink a beverage as you greet. This created a more relaxed approach to greeting without sacrificing a sense of warmth.

Whether your greeters shake hands with your guests is your call. But it's not an arbitrary one. This decision should flow out of your mission, your church's culture, your community, and your guests' responses. Ask yourself what you want them to say about their experience on Monday morning, *then* decide.

Place More People Than Signs

When I returned from my first Willow Creek conference, I talked for weeks about the attention that was lavished on the conference attendees. Greeters were out in force. It seemed that a smiling "How can I serve you?" servant was positioned every 30 feet or so. Obviously, this didn't happen by mistake.

Although there was adequate signage, volunteers were near stairs, doors, and other entryways to answer questions and offer assistance. Breaks ran smoothly, meals were served proficiently, and information was disseminated efficiently. The volunteer team was available to answer nearly any question, nearly anywhere in the building.

> Signs are necessary, but they can never replace people.

Signs are necessary, but they can never replace people. They merely announce what everyone will want to know at some point. But they are only visible when they are nearby. If guests are on the upper level of a building and the room they need is on the lower level, a sign is not likely to tell them this. However, if people on your team are adequately placed, guests can easily be directed to the location, regardless of the signage. Post signs, but position more people. (More about signage in chapter 8.)

Pay attention to volunteer-to-guest ratios. At Granger we estimate one guest services team member for every 60 guests. (This doesn't include the children's center, which has a far higher ratio of volunteers.) Consider the culture you're trying to create, and be true to your mission as you establish your own ratios.

More Than Passing the Plate

As I was growing up in a small, rural church, I thought the only thing an usher did was gather the offering. At our church there were usually four ushers: one on each outside aisle and two in the center. I thought it might be a fun job. "Boy, you'd have to be on your toes to remember which row the plate already went down. Wouldn't want to accidentally pass it twice," I thought. (Once, though, the plates *were* passed twice, on purpose! Apparently the preacher thought the crowd could have done better, so he had the ushers pass them around again!)

I've since learned that ushering is more than passing a plate; it's essential to ensuring a positive experience inside the auditorium.

As our guests approach our auditorium, they are greeted by ushers who provide them with programs. This is one of the easiest and most fun ways to serve in the guest services ministry. It's ideal for people who love people but aren't truly extroverted. They aren't the shyest people on the team by any means, but they may be less likely to answer a phone or approach a family or individual needing special attention. At the door they are confident in their role, as they offer a smile and a program.

Inside the auditorium, ushers in each aisle help guests find seats. Often our teams help guests well before vacant seats become scarce. We've found, as I'm sure you have, that families and friends who arrive together like to sit together. So when guests are escorted and directed to open seats early, the ushers can move people toward the front half of the room and toward the row centers, allowing people who arrive together to sit together. Additionally, once the service has begun, team members know where available seats are, because they've been working the aisles already.

In most churches, ushers also receive the offering. You can receive the offering nearly any way you'd like. At Granger, we've structured this process to be as sensitive to guests as possible.

First, the host or speaker introduces the offering in this general fashion: "We're now going to receive an offering. Many of you give generously every week because your lives have been changed by the love of God. You understand and support the value and work of this church in our community and around the world. So you give. I invite you today to do so again with generosity and thanksgiving to God."

He or she will frequently add, "Now, if that's not you, we didn't invite you here to get your money. We invited you here to hear the good news of Jesus. We're so glad you've joined us today. As the offering bag comes your way, you may want to drop in your welcome card. Otherwise, please sit back, relax, and enjoy this song [or other celebration element] as the ushers come to receive our offering."

This helps guests feel at home and reminds the congregation of the presence of guests. Regardless of your church's size, it's one more way to communicate to your people that you expect guests in your services and to remind your people to give to the work of Christ through the local church.

As the ushers at Granger pass the bags down the rows, they step back from the row each time so people don't feel their giving is being scrutinized. While ushers must pay attention to the offering as it is passed along, we don't want any guest to think the ushers' job is to monitor who participates. A simple step back, behind the row, helps to prevent this misperception.

When Babies Don't Make It to the Nursery

As your team understands how critical it is to be a part of the weekend service teams, they will step up to the difficult tasks associated with ushering. A crying baby can blow the "Wow!" for your guests in the middle of the service, and it's up to your usher team to prevent or minimize this distraction.

While families are an important focus in our ministry to guests, little ones can create a distraction for more than the parents during the service. What's the ushers' responsibility when babies cry, talk, and coo during the service?

At Granger we love families. We love children. It's why we created a state-of-the-art, interactive children's center. During every adult-oriented service, our children's center engages children in the story of Christ, using media, games, music, drama, lights, and play designed for their specific ages. We minister to the entire family in this way.

So guest services teams are trained to recognize families who would benefit from knowing about the offerings in our children's center. It is one of the primary functions of our campus guides team. We never tell families that their children are not allowed to be in the service with them. However, we provide a tour of the children's area, and we encourage parents to allow their children to participate with others their age.

If families choose to bring their children into the auditorium with them, we recommend they sit near the back of the room on an aisle.

This proactive process makes it less difficult to approach a parent whose child is not interested (indicated by restlessness, crying, talking, or the cutest jabber) in the service. Tension is reduced when rapport has been established and parents understand that our guest services team is available to help make their experience a positive one. Parents are then more likely to perceive assistance, such as showing them to children's classrooms or a viewing area outside the auditorium, as helpful. Ushering is an extension of hospitality that creates comfort and ease inside the auditorium.

> Ushering is an extension of hospitality that creates comfort and ease inside the auditorium.

Paying attention to these kinds of details will produce varying results in each local church. Give careful consideration to your current environment, with an eye toward your *desired* environment. What elements will you monitor, alter, add, or eliminate to create "Wow!" throughout each guest's entire experience?

Try These Next Steps...

- Review your senior leadership's commitment to a guest services ministry. If the level of commitment should be greater, what can you do to improve it? If it's already high, what can you do to celebrate it?

- Review each section titled "Your Opportunity," beginning on page 60, and note some action steps appropriate to your setting.

- Prioritize these opportunities. Which one will you pursue first?

5

The Hospitality Factor

"Give people the information to act; then look for magic to happen!"[1]

What You Know: That Is the Answer

Empower your teams with knowledge. Whether there are 2 or 200 people on your weekend guest services teams, they must be well informed. And believe me, they want to be empowered with the knowledge they need to do well.

My few years with a retail clothing company showed me the power of being well-informed. In fact, one afternoon in a store near Chicago, I understood clearly what a *lack* of information will do. I had been away from the business for over three years and was then on staff at Granger Community Church. But I was meeting a friend from the apparel company at this store, and I had some time to kill. Helping people is just in my blood, and I still adopt a "Can I help you?" posture when I visit the store. Steve, the store manager, saw me step in to help stock a box of belts that had just arrived, so when the next customer walked in, he looked at me with a big "let's see how you handle this" smile, nodded, and walked away!

I turned to the customer and greeted him. I navigated my way through the customer's inquiry, laid out a few ensembles, and handed the sale off to Steve. I must admit I felt pretty pleased with myself! Steve was with someone else when another customer walked in, so I greeted him and thought I'd just walk through another sale.

"I need a pair of burgundy leather shoes. Do you have any?"

I looked around in the obvious places. No burgundy shoes in sight.

"Steve..." I hesitated. Grinning, he handed me a catalog. I found no burgundy shoes. Then the gentleman asked for a suede jacket. Again I looked in the obvious places and searched the catalog. No suede jackets that I could see...

"Steve?"

"Yes, Mark," he teased. He was having too much fun at my expense! He was able to confirm that no suede jackets were available. As the customer began to ask his third question, I lobbed the responsibility for answering into Steve's court. This experience demonstrated all too clearly that a lack of knowledge means a lack of help.

A lack of knowledge means a lack of help.

Your guests have questions. They will ask, "Where's the restroom?" "Where's the room for 2-year-olds?" "Where do I sign up for the retreat?" Your team must be adequately equipped to help.

Your Evaluation: How well-informed are your people? If you have guest services teams, are they equipped with the knowledge they need to inform, direct, and answer questions? For instance, do your greeters know the locations of each of the children's rooms and what ages go to each room? Do your team members know how and to whom to direct inquiries? Is there a central, known location where guests can get the information they need?

Granger's Model: For a long time, we've recognized that the larger a church grows, the higher the demand for a system that gets information to the people who are responsible for disseminating it. We never stop working on this. We want guests to be able to access the information they need from guest services personnel. And we never want members of our guest services center team to have egg on their faces when asked a question.

To achieve this, we have committed to first coordinate with each of the ministries promoting their opportunities for connection and service. This requires tremendous interdependency.

Each of our ministries follows the same process for promotion and communicating details to their audience. Our communications team has developed a system using online tools that automatically places every promotion in the program, online, in a service slide, or other form of communication. Our guest services center team understands that our website is their friend. Information there resources them to answer questions, register guests, and direct them online for more information.

In addition, as we learn about guests' needs, we add to our "stuff to know" file, which contains answers to frequently asked questions. We encourage teams to delve into the questions and to review the information that others have gleaned.

Other "WOW!" Models: The few times I've needed to access Apple's help desk, their in-store Genius Bar, I've been impressed. The team is always knowledgeable, whether my question is about my phone, iPad, or Mac. They've always offered more than one approach to my problem, starting with no-cost solutions first.

I recently heard a similar story from an attendee in a workshop I was leading in southern Ohio. She'd called the "complaint department" of Apple but didn't really have a complaint. She merely needed help with a product. The associate didn't transfer her call; he didn't reply, "That's not my job." Additionally, he had been cross-trained and was well equipped to answer her questions. Her problem was resolved. She was happy. Apple had wowed again.

Your Opportunity: Where is the informational "black hole" in your church? Maybe it's time to set up an information center. Perhaps your next step is to form a team of people who love serving people, are excellent at follow-through, and communicate well. You may need to pull in some systems specialists to help you streamline the information pipeline from ministry teams to the information center.

Real Hospitality Is Personal

Some of the most enjoyable evenings I've spent with friends have begun with a tour of their homes. The Wegners are a good example. When I was first in Rob and Michelle's home, they gave me the grand tour— every room in the house. I heard stories about furniture, pictures, and toilet-training potty chairs. (Their teenage girls don't want those stories told here!) I was instantly an insider. I could confidently find my way to the bathroom or any other room in the house. I felt welcome to get a drink from the kitchen or change the channel on the television. Some "Wows" are impressive *because* they're simple and they're personal.

Some "Wows" are impressive *because* they're simple and they're personal.

Your Evaluation: Are guests being genuinely welcomed in your church? Who are the people on your team who begin conversations easily and, more important, know how to actively listen? What opportunities exist in your church for the development of this team or at least for this function to be fulfilled?

Granger's Model: When Granger's information center was in the "dog-ugly resource trailer" I described earlier, it was staffed by a team that oversaw a small resource table. However, as we made plans to move into our new auditorium in May 2000, brainstorming about guest services led to the creation of an additional team. When the auditorium was complete, our once tiny connection area became a spacious atrium lobby. With the vision for adequate connection space realized, not only were we *able* to offer better service but the new space *required* it.

Our atrium is situated between the main entry doors and the auditorium. As guests pass through this area, we wanted to offer more than information; we wanted to offer people. We wanted to be able to guide guests to the children's center. We wanted to engage in conversation. We wanted to be personal. We wanted to be hospitable. So we formed a team to focus on guest reception and information.

This team does what we could never do in our previous space. Before, our greeters barely managed to greet, offer programs, and direct guests to seats. The space was just too small to allow for much interaction.

Members of the new guest services center team initially fulfilled three primary functions. First, they staffed the information center, answering questions and offering assistance regarding next-step opportunities. Second, they staffed the small beverage area, which at that time consisted of a cooler of bottled beverages and automatic cappuccino and coffee machines. Finally, they were available to assist families and individuals throughout the building.

Today a fully staffed restaurant, called The Eatery, serves guest drinks, express snacks, salads, and sandwiches. Our team of campus guides provide personal assistance, escorting families to kids' classrooms and answering quiestions for newcomers

We've discovered some sure indicators to identify first-time visitors walking into the church. And we've taken the time to train our campus guides to engage our guests based on those indicators.

Consider this: On your first visit to a store, museum, or mall, what are the first things you do when you step inside? Your eyes roam as you take in the place. Your pace slows. You look for the restroom. (OK, *I* look for the restroom!) These are sure signs that you're new to a place or setting.

The same is true of people entering a church building. Our campus guides deliberately pick up on those clues and offer a welcome and an introduction. What often follows is the opportunity to exchange names, perhaps get a little acquainted, and then show the guests to places of interest.

When team members greet families with children, they may spend up to 15 or 20 minutes with them. I've heard great stories of connections that have been made during this critical time as families are shown to the children's center. At Granger, children travel from the upper level to their classrooms on the lower level via a tube slide while their parents continue conversation with their campus guide. Team members often reconnect with the parents after the service to answer questions, assist them in picking up their children, and lead them to the information center if appropriate.

Members of this team hang out near our guest services center to be available and accessible to new guests as they engage children's check-in and guest services teams. This team requires our most outgoing, personable team members. SHAPE and fit matter here!

While hospitality is the function of every guest services team at Granger, our guest services center team and our campus guides generally engage our guests most directly and personally. Our guest services team has been freed up from serving beverages and providing personal tours, allowing them to focus on inquiries, telephone calls, and registering guests for next-step events and activities.

Our campus guides provide a level of hospitality that other guest services teams cannot provide as easily because our guides are mobile, not stationed at any one post.

Other "Wow!" Models: On one occasion, as our family waited in a small, crowded waiting area at Carrabba's Italian Grill, a server offered us hors d'oeuvres—on the house! A few minutes after the first sampling, we were offered a second. Another round and we would have been too full to select any entrées!

A friend had suggested we might enjoy sitting at the kitchen bar during our meal. I normally choose to sit as far away from the bustle and clatter of the kitchen as possible. But on this particular evening, we were game for a new experience, so we asked for seats there. It was a hospitality treat! The chefs asked us about our tastes in food as we waited for the server to take our order. To help us decide, the kitchen crew served up *more* samples from the menu!

Throughout the meal we talked with the staff about their cooking experiences, their schedules, what they liked about their jobs. We got acquainted! We were invited in. We felt at home.

Your Opportunity: Hospitality can certainly be extended in any number of ways. *How* you engage in the ministry of hospitality will depend on your facility, your attendance, and your culture. *Who* you recruit to serve is critical. Team members must have outgoing personalities, the gifts of hospitality and/or helps, and the ability to attract people. It's imperative that they have the ability to read body language and begin conversations naturally.

Kill the Answering Machine— Especially on the Weekend

Pound/pound and zero/zero are two of my favorite combinations when reaching a business's automated phone line. I remember trying to reach a credit card company to ascertain my balance and close the account. The menu list had more options than a gambler in Las Vegas! It went on and on. Of course there was no option stating, "If you'd like to end your relationship with our company, please press 911." I spent three minutes navigating this maze, then I had to breathe deeply and calm down when I finally reached a live human voice.

Your Evaluation: What do your guests experience when trying to call your church on the weekend? Is anyone available to answer simple questions such as "What time does your service start?"

Granger's Model: Our guest services center team now answers the phone throughout every service, taking calls on subjects ranging from service times to crises. In this way we've been able to convey messages to volunteer servants and staff who would otherwise not have received important, urgent messages. And we've shown a friendly, hospitable face to all callers.

The weekend is *the* time to answer the telephone. Remember that it takes a special person to convey caring and understanding over the telephone. Put people on your phone lines who sound as personable over the phone as they do in your lobby or narthex.

Add the Janitor to the Guest Services Team

I'm actually not particularly picky…most of the time. My wife agrees with me but says that when I *am* picky, I am super picky. When browsing in a shop, I see the dust standing on the clothing rack, grime on the baseboard trim, smudges on the front window. The lack of cleanliness reflects poorly on the staff and the company. It's distracting to the whole experience. I don't think I'm the only one who notices such things.

Your Evaluation: Remember, your team's primary role is to identify potential distractions and proactively eliminate or minimize them. If your guests notice fingerprints on the front windows and doors, will this be what they're thinking about as they enter the building? If your guests find no toilet paper in the restroom, do you think they'll be distracted from the service they're about to attend? (The probable answer is "yes.")

Granger's Model: Our facility care director understands guest services. She has recruited a team of volunteers to do the housekeeping at Granger throughout the weekend. Their role is to keep the glass clean, particularly at the main entry doors; stock the restrooms and wipe down toilets, sinks, and mirrors; empty trash; keep airlocks free from rainwater and melting snow; and keep the carpeted floors in pristine condition.

Thanks to the collaboration of leadership, this team has joined the ushers and greeters in being an important part of our guest services team. Members wear name tags and are therefore visible and available to assist guests.

Other "Wow!" Models: My family and I were guests at Westwinds Community Church in Jackson, Michigan. The very mission of the church is woven into the design of the building. A journey through the church's corridors, lobby, and auditorium is intended to be spiritually affecting. Such an excursion must be free of distractions. Obviously Westwinds' core ministry, in a growing community of artists, is not that of "building services." However, the church has not overlooked this detail, and in fact, volunteers maintain the building daily. Extraordinary ministry is taking place in Jackson, Michigan, because first impressions really do matter to this church.

Your Opportunity: What will you do to remove encumbrances to your church's message? How will you make the housekeeping team part of your first impressions ministry? Do your support teams know they are part of your ministry to your guests? Are they embracing the vision to connect to people? Have you found ways to include every passion for connection, regardless of gifts, abilities, personalities, and experiences?

E very gift counts; count every gift a treasure!

Regardless of how they're wired to serve, allow people who love to see others connected become engaged in the process. Every gift counts; count every gift a treasure!

Try These Next Steps...

- What one change in your lobby could significantly improve the atmosphere for your guests? What would it take to make this change?

- How would adding a housekeeping team to your guest services ministry affect your weekend experience? Who is covering these details now?

- Review each section titled "Your Opportunity" beginning on page 73, and note some action steps appropriate to your setting.

Endnote

1. Ken Blanchard, John P. Carlos, and Alan Randolph, *Empowerment Takes More Than a Minute* (New York: MJF Books, 1996), 77.

6

Service Behind
the Scenes

---

*"Whatever you do, work at it with all your
heart, as working for the Lord, not for men."*
(Colossians 3:23)

Who's in Charge?

I've been involved in churches in which the leaders of guest services
ministries were strictly administrators. While administratively gifted people
can make superb leaders, the ability to establish organizational flowcharts
and schedules is not the leadership priority of a guest services ministry.
Along with demonstrated gifts of leadership, one must possess extraordinary
interpersonal skills. Because most guest services teams are made up
of people-oriented people, they need leaders who connect relationally.

True leaders genuinely value people. Leaders don't use people; they give
them the tools that enable them to succeed. When you look for leaders,
look for people who are looking out for others. Look for people who will
create an invigorating atmosphere—both on their teams and through
their teams. Recruit leaders who model warmth and approachability to
guests and teammates.

People with their hands held the highest,
begging for the lead role, don't get this job.
Jesus had something to say about this in
Mark 10. Two of his disciples, James and
John, got their heads together and made a
rather daring proposal to Jesus. They wanted

> **W**hen you look for
> leaders, look for
> people who are
> looking out for
> others.

Ideal servant-leaders are those who are willing but reluctant.

positions of honor at his left and right side. Jesus replied, "You have no idea what you're asking…Whoever wants to be great must become a servant. Whoever wants to be first among you must be your slave" (Mark 10:40, 43-44, The Message).

Jesus says leadership is about serving. It's about saying, "I'm third. I'll follow Jesus; I'll serve people; I'll be last." Jesus says everything rises and falls on leadership, and leaders fall to last place in order to rise to greatness in his kingdom.

Brett Eastman, founder of Life Together and former small-group guru at both Willow Creek Community Church and Saddleback Church, taught me that ideal servant-leaders are those who are willing but reluctant. They depend on God to lead. They value following as they lead. They build and involve teams. They know how to be third. When leaders demonstrate selflessness, team members do the same.

Your Evaluation: Based on these criteria, who do you know in your ministry who is leading but shouldn't be? Who do you know who is not leading but should be asked? How does third place feel to you?

Granger's Model: There are some fantastic people serving on teams who previously served as greeters in other churches. But we don't limit our selection to those with prior experience in church ministry. In fact, some of our most exceptional volunteer leaders are those who deliver customer service in the marketplace.

Consider Nancy. She coaches 12 usher/greeter leaders, who lead four teams totaling nearly 250 people. For over 25 years, she has worked in service industries. She understands systems and that systems serve people. She values teams and leads them with care. She makes guests a priority and builds great trust on her teams.

Carl and Zena are a husband-and-wife team who improve everything they touch. His marketplace experience in sales and management along with her experience in customer service combine for a total of 40-plus years of serving others in the marketplace. They love people. I've watched more people connect and connect quickly to Granger Community Church through their friendships than any other couple I know.

They call out the best in others. They carry vision that comes through in every action and conversation. Their intentional investment in individuals is nothing short of sacrificial and amazing.

After leading in our guest services ministry at our Granger campus for years, they accepted the invitation to oversee our teams at our first multisite in Elkhart, Indiana. They transferred working systems, built teams, and standardized excellence on our campus there. Their love for Jesus along with their marketplace leadership acumen have positioned them perfectly to lead as servants in our ministry.

Judy is a financial planner. Dennis and Joyce own their own hot tub business. Tonya is a pharmacist. Davis is a car dealership service manager. Shelly is a graphic and interior designer. Nate is an investment broker. Steve and Debbie are both in insurance and financial planning.

All of these people bring tremendous experience from their workplaces to their roles as servant-leaders. Not every leader manages or sells. But all good leaders love people; they value teamwork. They understand their role in fulfilling the church's mission statement. At the same time, leaders of these teams *do* need some organizational skills. At Granger we've developed a summary of the qualities and abilities necessary to lead our guest services ministries; it can be found in the reproducible handout "Guest Services Leaders Must..." at the end of this chapter (p. 92).

Invite people who appreciate third place to lead with you. Find people who are a bit reluctant but willing to give it a shot. Look for leaders who will build teams—to connect, to grow, to give, and to serve together. Tap their life and work experiences; God will use them all!

Your Opportunity: Who will you ask to help you create a place where guests will say "Wow!" in their first 10 minutes on your campus and, consequently, remain open to the message of Christ?

Not Everyone's an Extrovert

Not everyone must be a "people magnet" to serve your guests. Many folks in your church have a passion to connect people to God and to one another,

> **N**ot everyone must be a "people magnet" to serve your guests.

but they aren't wired to greet guests. Find a way to include them, for they, too, are invaluable to the success of a guest services ministry.

At Granger, a team of people gathers every Saturday afternoon to assemble between 5,000 and 10,000 pieces of paper for the weekend program. These people are part of our guest services team.

Our guest services teams serve extraordinary hours on their weekend rotations. On Saturday afternoon they arrive before 4:00 and serve until nearly 9:00 that evening, so they miss dinner. On Sundays they arrive by 8:00 in the morning and serve until after 1:00 in the afternoon. Can you feel the hunger?

To serve these people, a group of volunteers maintains table service and beverages for everyone who wants to eat.

You'll find a complete listing of all of our guest services teams in Chapter 3, on pages 47 and 48. But here in the box on the left, you'll find a sampling of opportunities that your quieter connectors might explore.

Connecting Behind the Scenes

Here are some ways that less gregarious members of your congregation can connect people to others and to God:

- Mail reminder postcards to team members.
- Purchase or prepare food for serving teams.
- Prepare programs for the weekend.
- Set out parking lot cones.
- Pray for the weekend teams and guests.
- Update team rosters and profiles.
- Coordinate systems that ensure all ministry information is gathered for the guest services center.
- Stock the guest services center with information and registration packets.

Nobody Plans an Emergency, but Everybody Needs a Plan

Nothing can destroy your guests' experience as quickly and thoroughly as an emergency—especially if an emergency response plan is not in place or is poorly executed. It may be tempting to minimize the need for precautionary measures because emergencies in the church are rare, but the risks of not being prepared are too great to ignore.

For example, what is your team trained to do if a parent or other relative picks up a child from a classroom without the custodial parent's permission? Who does what if the fire alarm sounds during a service? Where does everyone go if severe weather poses an immediate threat? What if the pastor is threatened or confronted during a service?

When an emergency occurs and no plan is in place, not only will guests be in danger, but their trust in your church will be shaken as well. Planning for emergencies is not only responsible, it is also expected by your guests. After all, their children's schools have emergency response plans, their workplaces have protocol, and their malls have procedures. Churches must be equally prepared.

For all of these reasons, it's vital that your church plans a response to each of the following scenarios.

Child Abduction

Stories of abducted children abound. No community is immune to the threat posed by a determined relative who has been denied access to his or her child. Many churches utilize a check-in system that requires people to display some form of matching document, tag, or bar code before children may be released into their custody. But what happens when someone attempts to take a child without this authorization?

Combative Persons

Armed or unarmed, a threatening person in your church building must be restrained. A plan should be in place to ensure no one is hurt during verbal or physical confrontations. Develop a written plan explaining how to talk to and behave toward a combative person until security personnel or police arrive.

Fire

A screeching fire alarm in a room or building of any size will cause panic and confusion unless people are prepared for it. A strategic plan involving children's teams, guest services teams, and auditorium service producers will minimize confusion and allow for an orderly evacuation if one is needed.

Severe Weather

Your guests don't know where the safest places in your building are. It's likely that a lot of long-time members don't even know. A plan to monitor websites and radio bulletins during severe weather alerts and to move everyone to safe locations will help assure that everyone finds shelter during severe weather.

Theft

When devising a plan to prevent theft, include the following questions in your consideration: How visible are your ushers when carrying the offering plates or bags from the auditorium? What policies are in place for separating, counting, and depositing money? Implementing preventive measures will help you avoid theft of any kind.

Medical Emergencies

No one can predict a medical emergency. Heart attacks, maternal labor, and cuts and contusions from falls are common anytime a crowd of any size gathers. Trained professionals such as nurses, physicians, firefighters, and emergency medical technicians probably attend your church and would be happy to be part of a medical response team if you ask them.

Developing an Emergency Response Plan

At Granger we developed an all-inclusive emergency response plan by collaborating with a number of emergency and law-enforcement professionals, most of whom attend our church. The roundtable included a fire chief, a police officer, our facility care director, our director of children's ministries, our guest services director, and myself. After a series of meetings to identify threats, needs, responses, and appropriate roles for individual teams, those with administrative gifts saw the project through to completion (i.e., not me). Our Emergency Response Manual, which undergoes periodic updates, may be purchased at wiredchurches.com.

Your local fire and police departments will probably be happy to offer you the consulting support you need to implement a plan that addresses your unique setting. These organizations emphasize prevention; don't hesitate to ask for their help.

After developing your plan, be sure every member of your guest services ministry is thoroughly trained to implement it. Because emergencies are rare, people will forget how to respond without ongoing training and retraining. Require members of each team to spend a few minutes each week reviewing their responsibilities in the event of an emergency.

Developing a Safety Team

Our safety plan specifically addresses the threats listed earlier: child abduction, combative persons, and theft. Although we call 911 in any of these situations, we also rely on people on the campus who are trained to minimize or avert the danger these situations pose.

In developing a safety team, we initially recruited only those in our church family who were trained law enforcement officers. For a variety of reasons, including scheduling issues, we soon experienced attrition that jeopardized coverage. We had to rethink how to staff our newly developed safety team.

First we identified qualified leaders, and this has been the key to the team's success. For years now, this team has been led by volunteers. The team consists of people with both formal and informal training. Our leaders bring competence and confidence to their leadership roles—essentials in establishing trust and teamwork.

This team's primary responsibility is to provide a calm, reassuring, approachable presence in the face of a threat. Second, they are trained to be aware of suspicious circumstances and behavior. They are trained to watch, to pick up on anything abnormal. They walk through the entire building before services, looking for suspicious items. They roam the children's center, parking lots, and atrium.

Members of this team generally wear sport coats; in our specific setting, this reflects an appropriate level of authority and professionalism. Badges or police-style "security" shirts wouldn't be appropriate in our culture. As you form your safety team, be sure its members are aligned with your church's philosophy of ministry. Set clear expectations for how they will present themselves in appearance and demeanor.

Developing a Medical Team

Dr. Alan Snell was serving as a greeter one weekend at Granger when a guest's chest pains seemed to indicate a heart attack. Needless to say, everyone was grateful for Alan's training and expertise. As a result of that experience, Alan asked to develop a team to respond to future medical emergencies.

When a gifted leader expresses a passion to direct an area of ministry, we give the green light.

When a gifted leader expresses a passion to direct an area of ministry, we give the green light. Alan began to tap the shoulders of medical professionals within our church, and today nearly 40 volunteers serve on this team on a rotating basis. Training is standardized for every participant, regardless of his or her skill level. Each team member is trained in basic CPR and in the use of an automated external defibrillator (AED), an Epi-Pen (used to treat reactions to bee stings and other minor allergies), and supplemental oxygen.

Although Dr. Snell has moved from our area, the team is strong. At every service, four to five of these team members each pick up a vibrating beeper from the guest services team and are available throughout that hour. Nearly every weekend, at least one of them is called upon to respond to a medical need. Medical team members are thrilled to use their skills and training to serve people in the church.

Your church undoubtedly has people who can provide the necessary resources, training, and leadership to ensure that people receive competent intermediate care while waiting for a 911 response.

Who's in Charge of Communication?

As our church grew, it became increasingly necessary to have one person in charge of communication during each service. This person is command central. All emergencies and special needs are communicated to this point person; he or she in turn communicates each need to the appropriate team. In the event of an emergency, the point person coordinates the church's response to the entire event, using carefully scripted announcements to give direction to the congregation.

Point persons are the keepers of the Emergency Response Manual; they must know it thoroughly. On each of our campuses, point persons and other weekend leaders communicate via radio headsets. The point person's primary role is to keep systems running smoothly by communicating accurately and thoroughly. In addition, the person assists other leaders as needed, serving as gofer, greeter, or additional safety personnel.

Servants Must Be Wowed Too

Over time, even the most gregarious people can begin to view their role of extending a warm welcome and exuding acceptance as a task—a duty—and miss out on the very community they hope to build. And other factors, such as strained family relationships, stress at work, and unrest with God, can drain them of the ability to extend genuine acceptance to guests. For real community to exist, people have to slow down, share a cup of coffee, and talk about who they really are.

An important challenge for the leader of a guest services ministry, then, is to cultivate a culture that encourages team members to explore their hearts rather than just concentrate on tasks. When conversation reaches this level, people more genuinely affirm one another. As they are affirmed as the unique treasures God made them to be, they begin to see their guests in the same way. This shift in focus recharges their commitment to the ministry, and authentic acceptance flows from them again.

Our team members used to serve in one service a month. They would take a stack of bulletins and stand at the doors to which they were assigned. Or they would participate in the service, wait for offering time, then stand and receive the offering. It was entirely possible for many of them to not even know the other members of their teams. They missed any chance of serving together in community. The ministry was focused on tasks, not connections.

That's why we developed a new rotation schedule, asking teams to serve all evening Saturday, all morning Sunday, or *all* weekend every four weeks. Their reporting time is not five minutes before the service starts, but an hour to 90 minutes beforehand. During that hour-plus time period, team members meet, talk, share Scripture, pray together, and help one another prepare to serve our guests. Leaders make serving assignments, answer questions, review the emergency response plan, and review best practices.

We also provide a place for team members to visit with one another when they have some "down time" during the service. They can share a meal and talk. They can connect with one another as they serve together.

Teams also spend time together apart from their serving weekends. Leaders organize barbeques and other gatherings to further enhance community.

And our guests are the indirect beneficiaries. The acceptance that guests feel as they step onto our campus isn't manufactured; it's a contagious attitude that begins with team members' acceptance of one another!

We have learned that community *can* be experienced in this ministry. It's a shame if it isn't.

Try These Next Steps...

- If a weather-related, medical, or fire emergency occurred at your church this week, what's the worst-case scenario? Who in your church or community can help you outline an emergency response plan within the next 60 days?

- Who coordinates communication between ministry areas on the weekends? Is anyone bridging the gaps between the ministries to children, youth, guests, and the people in the auditorium? How connected do these teams feel to a common vision and mission for the weekend services?

- If your teams are established, to what degree are the people serving on them connected with one another? How is community encouraged? How many of the people on your greeting team are connected to other friendships, groups, or teams? If you're just initiating this ministry, how will you build a sense of community within these teams?

- Review the section titled "Your Opportunity" on page 83, and note some action steps appropriate to your setting.

Guest Services Leaders Must...

- Actively support the mission, vision, values, and purposes of Granger Community Church.

- Complete core membership classes, defining and expressing their unique SHAPE in ministry.

- Model Mark 10:43 ("Whoever wants to become great among you must be your servant") and Philippians 2:5 ("Your attitude should be the same as that of Christ Jesus").

- Develop other leaders by (a) mentoring others with an eye toward being replaced by them and (b) delegating various responsibilities to others who will assist them in leading their teams.

- Train all team members before and after group training through on-the-job training that is often just-in-time training (that is, training on the weekend, just as the team member needs to know it).

- Deliver guest services on assigned weekends.

- Recruit team members to serve on assigned weekends.

- Act as liaison between the point person and their teams, demonstrating cooperation and clear communication, particularly during emergencies.

- Provide ongoing feedback to their volunteer coordinators and/or staff directors.

7

Training for the Experience

"Successful teams are those that understand that the desired end product is transformation, not transactions."[1]

Train the Heart First; the Details Will Follow

As you prepare your teams for ministry, training is critical. But before you address the details of delivering excellent service, you must cement some foundational building blocks within your team members. As you're laying this foundation, I encourage you to emphasize *principles* and *values*. Rather than presenting a 99-page how-to manual, paint a broad-stroke picture of the atmosphere you want to create.

If your teams get too caught up in completing their ministry assignments correctly without first engaging their hearts in the mission, your environment will be characterized by performers of tasks. The atmosphere may be efficient, but it will likely be chilly as well. Cast vision; teach the mission of your church and ministry; describe clear objectives. Then invite your teams to help create an environment in which these objectives can be met.

> Rather than presenting a 99-page how-to manual, paint a broad-stroke picture of the atmosphere you want to create.

A Road Map for Training Your Guest Services Team

The purpose of initial training is to give members of your guest services team the opportunity to agree with the ministry's objectives and understand how they can be a part of it. It's helpful to have the energy of critical mass as you define the ministry's vision, mission, values, purposes, and style. Your definition of *critical mass* will depend on your circumstances, but I've found that the more people, the better. I recommend you schedule two to three hours for this training, especially for larger groups. I also suggest that during this training, you set aside time every 10 to 15 minutes for people to interact within smaller groups. This will allow them to connect relationally, coach each other, and align with your ministry philosophy in a deeper, more personal way.

In the following pages, I'll outline a road map for group training. I encourage you to modify it as much as necessary to fit your church's unique culture and your personal training style.

The Power of First Impressions

Help your teams grasp the implications of our society's consumer culture. Start by using the exercise "First Impressions Last" on page 22 to help your teams grasp the indelible nature of first impressions. Then allow time for team members to talk about where they shop, the businesses and products to which they are loyal, and their own "Wow!" experiences, as well as disappointments they've experienced. This discussion will help your team members better understand your guests' expectations when coming to your church.

Your Ministry's Mission, Vision, and Values

Summarize your ministry's purpose and methods for helping guests feel welcome and safe. Encourage trainees to share personal stories about how they came to Christ and the church. If you want to adopt the "first 10 minutes" principle as a hallmark of your ministry, this is an ideal time to explore that idea.

If you are just beginning this ministry in your church, I recommend asking members of your senior staff or governing board to participate in this stage of training. If you are not the senior pastor, you might consider giving some of this teaching time to your senior leader. The significance of his or her voice in casting vision and cultivating an "others matter" culture will catalyze your ministry launch or improvements.

Remember What It's Like to Be a Guest

One weakness plaguing many of us is the tendency to forget. It's so easy to forget what it's like to be a guest in a new, unfamiliar setting. This forgetfulness weakens our ability to meet our guests with welcoming acceptance right where they are.

Jesus knows we have trouble with forgetfulness. It might be one reason he gave us the golden rule: "Do to others what you would have them do to you" (Matthew 7:12). If we forget what we once needed in a difficult situation, we're less likely to be empathetic toward others who need the same thing. For instance, if I had forgotten what it's like to be a young child during an electrical storm, I would have likely been annoyed when my then-5-year-old daughter came to my bedside at 1 o'clock in the morning after she had been startled by thunder! If I forget the kindness someone showed me in merging traffic just yesterday, I may refuse to let a driver move in front of me when I'm in a rush today.

> **I**t's so easy to forget what it's like to be a guest in a new, unfamiliar setting.

However, when we *remember* how it feels to be included rather than alienated, we're more likely to be inclusive. When we remember what it's like to need help without knowing where to find it, we're more likely to be helpful. When we remember our own spiritual hunger and search for fulfillment, we'll be more sensitive to our guests' needs for the same things.

Who Is Our Guest?

Try this exercise to help members of your team close the gap between how they view themselves and how they view your church's guests.

You'll need

- photocopies of the "Who Is Our Guest?" handout (p. 108)
- 4 to 6 recently submitted, anonymous prayer requests
- small cards or paper
- a backpack weighted with several books or bricks
- poster board or newsprint
- markers

Preparation: Prior to the training session, collect four to six actual prayer requests from people in your church. Your church's weekend comment cards, website, or prayer telephone line may be excellent sources. Removing any names from the requests, print them on individual cards or small strips of paper, and place them in a pocket of the backpack.

Form groups of four to six. Distribute markers, a sheet of poster board or newsprint, and a photocopy of the "Who Is Our Guest?" handout to each group. Give groups 8 to 10 minutes to discuss the questions on the handout and illustrate their conclusions. Then have each group share its "guest profile" with the other trainees. Celebrate each profile with hearty applause.

Debrief the entire group's conclusions, pointing out

• recreational activities common to your area;

• shopping trends;

• shared values;

• demographics related to age, marital status, children, and sometimes income ranges; and

• basic hopes, needs, and fears.

This exercise will demonstrate two things to the people in the training session. First, they know more about the people in their community than they might have realized. Second, these guests are very much like them; in fact, they have a lot in common.

Pass the backpack around the group, asking several people to select a prayer concern from the pocket and read it aloud.

As your team feels the weight of the pack and listens to concerns related to divorce, death, unemployment, and fears, suggest how this illustrates the burdens your guests carry as they enter your church. Behind the smiles are people with real needs, looking for real answers. Many, if not most, want to say, "Help me. I need something, someone, to help me with life."

Ask your group, "How many of you have carried at one time, or are now carrying, these kinds of concerns, questions, and fears?" Every hand in the room will go up. And the gap between team member and guest will evaporate, because your team will remember. This is one way to tap their hearts and help them be better prepared to create an environment of grace, warmth, and welcome.

HELLO: An Overview

Here's a simple acronym that's easy to remember, captures the essence of the relational environment a guest services ministry is intended to create, and generates lots of fun in training: HELLO. It outlines a natural progression of personal interaction with guests, leading them to think, "Wow! I'm impressed!"

As you explore each letter of the acronym, be sure to cite examples from your own experience as well as soliciting stories from the participants. Then, before moving to the next letter of the acronym, form groups of three. Have members of each trio choose a role: a guest, a greeter, or an observer. (Everyone will eventually rotate within the group, playing each of the three roles.) Ask each trio to role-play the letter of the acronym under discussion. This part of the activity goes very quickly.

Allow time for each trio to debrief the role-play, encouraging the members to delve more deeply into their perspectives as observer, guest, and greeter. Some of the best teaching will happen during this self-guided discussion. Remember that most of your team members are "people persons." They will teach and coach one another as they work through the activity.

Finally, take a few minutes to lead the entire group in a discussion, asking for highlights of each group's observations.

After you've completed this process for all five letters of the acronym, allow the groups to do a final role-play, using the entire acronym.

Have fun with this! It's a tool for teaching both a *principle* and a *technique* that will empower your team members to engage guests simply and sincerely. It will help your teams communicate that your guests matter to God, and therefore to you!

Although this five-step process might seem formulaic, it's really as organic as any conversation. Train with this five-piece focus, and your teams can engage every guest individually and consistently.

I've written the following text in the first person, as if I were facilitating the training session. Again, I urge you to customize your training by using all or part of this material in a way that will work best in your church's unique setting.

H is for "Hello"

Let's say you walk into a store at the mall, browse for a few minutes, find the item you're looking for, and proceed to the counter. Of course, you're expecting to pay for your merchandise and be on your way.

You reach the counter. "Good," you think, "someone's actually at the counter. What a great store." You're ready to complete the transaction. The sales associate is not. Something appears to be more important to her than you, a paying customer. You fidget as she leafs through a notebook, receipts in hand. She looks busy, even a little concerned. You sigh, shift your weight to your other foot, and push your merchandise two inches closer to her. Nothing. You're invisible.

You just want to be acknowledged. You'd like for her to simply say, "Hi! It's good to see you. Give me a second to clear this out of the way, then I'll be right with you."

The *H* in H-E-L-L-O is for, well, "hello." It's about acknowledgment, recognition. "Good morning!" "Hi!" "How are you?" Regardless of the wording, the acknowledgment simply means "I'm paying attention; I see you."

But your assignment as a greeter is not to be a handshaking "hello machine." This is about being observant and cordial. Eye contact is essential. If a guest makes eye contact with you, you must acknowledge him or her with an oral greeting, a pat, or a wave.

> **We must be fully present, focused on the moment and on each person in that moment.**

(At this point in the training, you might refer to the tips in Chapter 4 about learning to read body language. This is a great opportunity to do some impromptu role-playing.)

As we greet our guests, we must be fully present, focused on the moment and on each person in that moment. There will be other times to focus on your teammates and friends in the church. As important as those connections are, when you're serving, your attention must be on guests.

Have you ever gone into a store looking for a specific item? Let's say you want a light blue, button-down, cotton shirt. To expedite your search, you're prepared to ask someone for help. As you enter the store, you see three sales associates on one side of the store talking, laughing, and having a good time. Their circle is closed. On the other side of the room is a sales associate, standing alone, folding sweaters.

Whom would you approach: the three associates in a conversation or the associate folding sweaters?

That's right, you'd go to the person folding clothing. Why? Because he's approachable, he's present in the moment, he's open to your question. You wouldn't address the others because you might feel rude for interrupting them.

So, team, bust up your party! To acknowledge our guests, you must convey openness. A guest may want to ask a question. If you're engrossed in a conversation with a friend, the guest probably won't ask.

(Now it's your turn. Lead your group through the role-play as suggested on page 97.)

E is for "Engagement"

When you engage a guest, you move the encounter from a cordial recognition to a personal conversation that might include introductions, question-asking, and information-giving. As the greeter, your body language is critical in this step. Expressing genuine interest through your eyes and other gestures makes any conversation more engaging.

To show genuine interest, you need to slow down. This isn't easy for most of us. We always seem to have some place to be, some task to complete. Slowing your pace will help you to be present in the moment; it reminds you that people are your focus. When you pause to look people in the eye, you communicate that you have time for them.

When you pause to look people in the eye, you communicate that you have time for them.

A guest might engage you because you're wearing an official-looking name tag. Or you might take the initiative to engage a guest. For example, you might approach a young mother whose arms are full of children and diaper bags. Or perhaps you recognize that "I'm new here" pause by the family who just walked through the door. When you initiate a conversation, you've engaged the guest.

Regardless of who initiates the conversation, personalize it by introducing yourself. Maybe you've discovered this phenomenon: Nearly every time you introduce yourself to others, they will respond by voluntarily telling you their names. At this point, you're no longer strangers.

Having established this warmer level of engagement, new doors can be opened within the conversation. These guests now have a personal contact at your church. If they wanted or needed to, they could now ask for someone by name. This diminishes their sense of being outsiders.

Deepen the connection by addressing the guests' children with warmth and acceptance. As you meet your guests' families, kneel so you're at eye-level with younger children. Ask about names, ages, and interests. Be sure to introduce the family to the children's ministry team in the children's respective classrooms. By the time the parents are settled in the auditorium, their trust in your church's ability to care for their children should be established.

Don't try to force conversation or prolong it. Typically, the guest who wants immediate help or dialogue will take it from there. Set the stage for a natural exchange; if it doesn't happen organically, it is counterproductive.

Although you may quickly approach someone whose body language says, "I'm new here. Please help me," asking all the people who enter your church if they need help is like a restaurant host asking for your food order as soon as you walk through the door. Your objective is not to engage every person in prolonged discussion; it is to create a welcoming atmosphere so that when you do engage a guest, the exchange is warm, authentic, and personal.

(Now it's your turn. Lead your group through the role-play as suggested on page 97.)

L is for "Listen"

You've probably heard that God gave each of us one mouth and two ears because he wants us to listen at least twice as much as we talk. I don't know if that was his design, but human relationships are improved when we practice it!

Appropriate eye contact is critical to effective listening. Communication expert Bert Decker says that eye contact can communicate three "I's": involvement, intimacy, or intimidation. He says 5 to 10 seconds of eye contact followed by glancing away is generally a comfortable amount of time to establish involvement. Making eye contact for longer periods of time may communicate either intimacy or intimidation.[2] By making appropriate eye contact, you'll involve the guest, while maintaining a comfortable environment. Listening while making appropriate eye contact also communicates interest, empathy, and focus.

Your eyes certainly communicate connection, but the rest of your body language says plenty about your interest as well. For instance, crossing your arms while listening can convey "blocking," a barrier that demonstrates a lack of interest or, worse, resistance. Leaning against a wall, away from a person, can convey a lack of involvement. And listening with your hands on your hips can be quite intimidating.

Your posture should be relaxed and open. I encourage you to keep your hands in front of you rather than behind your back. If you're standing, avoid placing both hands in your pockets; this can be interpreted as "closed," in the same way as crossing your arms. Standing approximately two feet from your guests creates a fair sense of safety. However, as you read their body language, allow them to set their own personal space; then honor that boundary.

Miscommunication is often the result of poor listening. Listening actively requires focus and practice. Most of us are often too busy to listen well. When we ask in passing, "How are you?" we really don't want to hear the long, true answer. But when we stop, make appropriate eye contact, and focus on the moment, we offer our guests a huge gift.

(Now it's your turn. Lead your group through the role-play as suggested on page 97.)

L is for "Listen Some More"

While listening actively requires less talking, we do need to respond to ensure we're hearing what the other person is communicating. Asking questions and restating what you think you heard are listening skills that require time and practice to develop.

Here's an example of poor listening skills that led to unfortunate consequences. A woman, whom we'll call Janie, entered a Protestant church on a Saturday evening, found a greeter, and asked, "What time is Mass this evening?"

The greeter, whom we'll call Beth, assumed Janie had a grasp on religious vocabulary and assumed her question should be interpreted literally. She replied, "We don't have Mass this evening."

Janie left the building. Did she leave because she really wanted to attend Mass in a Catholic church? Or did she leave because she thought there were no more services that evening? We'll never know. Had Beth slowed down, made no assumptions, and listened actively by asking a clarifying question before answering, the conversation might have gone something like this:

"What time is Mass this evening?"

"Hi! Welcome. Let me make sure I understand what you're asking. By the way, my name is Beth."

At this point Janie would likely have introduced herself, and these women would have been on a first-name basis.

"Well, Janie, are you asking about a Catholic Mass, the Lord's Supper, or the time of our service this evening?"

Then Janie might have answered, "Oh, sorry. I don't know what you call it. I grew up Catholic. I'm just wondering what time your service—or Mass or whatever it's called—starts." Or she may have said, "Oh, I'm looking for Communion at a Catholic Mass." In either case Beth would have known what Janie really wanted and could have directed her appropriately.

Beth failed to ask questions and restate what she thought she heard. This kind of miscommunication doesn't have to happen in a guest services ministry. Asking questions clarifies facts, reveals feelings, and opens the door to rapport. Restating what we think we've heard allows speakers to correct us or to affirm that they've been listened to well. Both skills are essential to a successful guest services ministry.

(Now it's your turn. Lead your group through the role-play as suggested on page 97.)

O is for "Offer Assistance"

Once you've established that you understand your guest's need, you're ready to offer assistance. Of course, how you provide that help will depend on your assigned responsibility and the nature of the need. You may be serving at a post you can't leave. Perhaps you're serving at the guest services center; will other guests not be served if you escort a family to the children's center?

When responding to a guest's request, remember these two priorities: First, if you can offer the assistance personally, do it. Either your post can be abandoned for a short time, or you can find another team member to temporarily take your place. Second, if you must rely on another team member to assist your guest, introduce the guest to your teammate. Do not require your guest to repeat his or her request. Rather, explain what is needed, assuring your guest that he or she is in competent hands.

In either case, never point guests toward their destinations. Always escort them or see that someone else does. Whether they want to get to the children's center or the bookstore or the restroom, always take them; never point the way.

Have you ever asked for directions to a restroom or a particular product in a large department store? "Just follow this aisle to that pink blouse there on the corner. See it? Turn left, go to the green carpet, follow that to the right until you get to the lingerie. You'll see an elevator on the left. Take the elevator to the second floor, and follow the red and white tile through the appliances section. Then turn right and go to…"

"Huh?"

Always stop what you're doing and escort guests to their destinations. Never point, never direct, regardless of how close the destination is or how easy it is to find. People are wowed when this kind of personal attention is given to them. They are surprised that people care enough to take this much time.

George Soper is a senior vice president at Memorial Hospital in South Bend, Indiana. He has helped position Memorial as one of the top-ranking hospitals in customer satisfaction in the nation. He suggests ending every conversation with a guest with this fairly standard question: "Is there anything else I can help you with today?" But then George adds, "Because I have time." This phrase is simple, but it is truly profound.

> **"Is there anything else I can do to help you today? Because I have time."**

No phrase communicates more value to guests. "Is there anything else I can do to help you today? Because I have time." Try it.

(Now it's your turn. Lead your group through the role-play as suggested on page 97.)

Branding

Help your trainees understand the importance of consistency by discussing the concept of branding. Ask them with what organizations they identify the following words or symbols:

- swoosh
- red and white bull's eye
- golden arches
- Whopper
- latte

If they identified these symbols with the following companies, then someone's done their job: Nike, Target, McDonald's, Burger King, and Starbucks. See how a clearly defined brand ensures name recognition?

With name recognition comes reputation. If every pair of shoes you've bought from Nike has been comfortable, durable, and affordable, then Nike has credibility with you. Conversely (no pun intended), if you've been consistently disappointed by a certain brand, your experience will probably prevent you from buying that brand again.

When guests talk about your church at their workplace on Monday morning, they describe its reputation. Those who have not been to your church have it defined for them by someone else's experience.

A local church's reputation evolves and is cemented when every team on every weekend meets the same standard of excellence. That's consistency. During their four-week rotations, if Granger's team members created their own culture, handled the guest services center in their own way, or served guests in the bookstore by their own individual standards, there would be no consistency. The stories at the office from one Monday to the next wouldn't match. The church would develop a reputation for unreliability. Guests would not be satisfied, much less engaged.

Consistency is also vital because of the "rule of representation." According to this rule, when a guest encounters any one individual in an organization, he or she has encountered the organization itself.

This rule was illustrated to my wife and me a few years ago at the Sawgrass Marriott in Jacksonville, Florida. As the bellman, Steve, assisted us with our luggage, he chatted with us about our trip, our family, and our marriage. As we talked, he learned we were celebrating our 21st anniversary. That evening, Steve had a basket of fruit, chocolates, and a bottle of champagne sent to our room. We were wowed!

The following year, we were guests at the Westin Hotel in Indianapolis. When Garfield, the director of marketing and sales, discovered we were celebrating our 22nd anniversary, he responded in much the same way. At 5 o'clock that evening, we were surprised by a knock on the door. We were treated to chocolate-covered strawberries and a chilled bottle of bubbly.

A tremendous resource we use in our training comes from the folks at Charthouse Learning. They've worked with the team at Seattle's world-famous Pike Place Fish Market to produce a delightful video training guide called FISH! (Visit fishphilosophy.com for ordering information.) This training video will revolutionize your team, helping team members understand the power of branding to create new "Wow!" experiences for your guests.

In both cases an individual went out of his way to make us feel especially valued. My wife and I still talk about how thoughtful it was of the Marriott and the Westin to treat us so splendidly. To Laura and me, Steve *was* the Marriott, and Garfield *was* the Westin.

When guests encounter any individual on your guest services team, they encounter your church. We tell our team members, "You *are* Granger Community Church. When you smile, our guests will leave thinking, 'What a pleasant church!' When you wow people with your listening skills and service, they will know that this is a church that cares. You *are* the church."

Of course, this is also true of negative experiences. If one greeter is indifferent, doesn't really listen, or doesn't follow through, the guest naturally assumes that the church is cold and uncaring.

Here's the good news: When you select people who are *SHAPEd* for this ministry and you train them, value them, and lead them, you will have a brand that consistently honors the name of Christ, and this reputation will be confirmed every Monday morning.

This Is Not About Cloning!

When we talk about branding, we're not talking about cloning. The goal is not to instill robotic behavior; it is to instill ownership and consistency. When every member of your team buys into the mission, vision, values, and purposes of your ministry, this personal ownership will be expressed in unique ways, but the overall experience—of welcome, caring, and warmth—will be consistent. Paul says in 1 Corinthians 12:7, "Each person is given something to do that shows who God is: Everyone gets in on it, everyone benefits. All kinds of things are handed out by the Spirit, and to all kinds of people! The variety is wonderful" (The Message).

Protect and encourage the authenticity of your teams. Unique personalities are tremendous assets on every team. When your teams own the ministry because they are wired to serve there, "Wows" will happen.

Consistency Happens Through Ongoing Training

As I stated earlier, I recommend you set aside a block of time to provide training on everything we've discussed to this point in this chapter. However, the vast majority of your team training will occur outside of this structured group time. True consistency and quality will emerge during on-the-job and just-in-time training.

Sometimes on-the-job and just-in-time training may be done in very small groups, but most of the time this level of training should occur one-on-one. It should happen relationally, on the spot, and should always include high levels of praise.

You may want to take advantage of an additional resource available at wiredchurches.com, our ministry resourcing arm of Granger Community Church. "Guest Services: Creating 'Wow' Experiences Training Videos" is a three-chapter training tool that may serve your teams well. These 20- to 40-minute segments offer best practices based on this book and my third book, *How to Wow Your Church Guests: 101 Ways to Make a Meaningful First Impression.* At Granger we're using it to establish a baseline of expectations and best practices in guest services and every other ministry of the church.

Celebration as Training

Praise is great one-on-one, when no one else is looking, but be sure to also honor your teams in large-group celebration events. Every year we throw a big party for all of our guest services teams. We spend an evening celebrating teams, individuals, and our collective ministry. We give awards based on humorous happenings, extreme commitment, and over-the-top guest service. It's a great opportunity to recast vision and lay out a road map for the upcoming year.

Take the time. Love your people. Celebrate them and honor them!

Try These Next Steps...

- What perceptions do your core members currently have of your guests?

- What could you do to help them see your guests differently, as they really are?

- If every guest were acknowledged without being smothered, how would that compare to what is happening now?

Endnotes

1. Laurie Beth Jones, *Teach Your Team to Fish* (New York: Crown Business, 2002), 111.

2. Bert Decker, as quoted in *50 Powerful Ideas You Can Use to Keep Your Customers* by Paul R. Timm (Franklin Lakes, NJ: Career Press, 2002), 45.

Who Is Our Guest?

Use the questions below as a springboard for defining our church's typical guest. Think of people such as your neighbors, friends, co-workers, workout partners, and the families of your children's friends. Choose an "artist" or two from your group to illustrate the group's answers, creating as complete a "profile" as possible.

- What does this person do for a living?

- What does he or she do for fun?

- Where does he or she shop? What is important to this person when shopping?

- Who are his or her friends? How deep are these friendships?

- How old is this person?

- What is his or her marital status?

- Does this person attend school? Where? What's his or her focus?

- What about family? Does this person have children? If so, what schools do they attend? In what other activities do they participate?

- What are this person's goals and dreams?

- Why did he or she come to church last weekend?

- What's on this person's mind? What are his or her worries and fears?

- What needs might this person verbalize to others?

8

Printed Impressions: Reading Between the Lines

"A brand must be so consistent that consumers experience it as coming from a company with a soul."[1]

Your Guests Are Reading You

Your printed material is part of your guests' overall experience, often their first experience with your church. You need to define this part of the experience, and you need to define it before the experience occurs.

Printed programs, fliers, signs, and logos are only words unless they communicate a vision. What goes in print must begin with the *purpose* of the church. Maurilio Amorim, CEO of the A Group, a media, technology, and branding firm in Brentwood, Tennessee, observes: "Before we can begin to build a brand, we must know our branding statement and position. 'We are a church; that's our position,' you might argue. But within the category of churches, yours should have its own identity, calling, niche, passion, or however you want to define your uniqueness. That's a deliberate message you need to continue to share, and it should always come through in your communication strategy."

Certainly people create atmosphere. But before your guests ever meet anyone at your church, they see your sign, they surf your website, or they read about you in their newspaper or your fliers. Upon arriving on your campus, your guests will "read you" further in every printed piece in your building. Will what they read be what they get?

Of course your church name matters, but that's likely already established. In addition to your name, how is your church identified in print? How and where does this show up? If you have a church logo, what does it communicate? What does your signage communicate? What does your other printed material convey? What do your guests intuit when they read these things? Is your church's true face recognizable in them?

What's in print may also be the impression that lingers as your guests take home your weekend programs or other ministry fliers. Your printed words either speak in place of a live person or they augment what your church has already communicated in other ways. When your guests read you, they will interpret what is important to your church. Amorim adds: "[W]e must remember that as far as the church is concerned, marketing is simply communication. Jesus commanded us in Luke 14:23 to go into the highways and lanes and 'compel' them to come in. And for marketing to build a brand, it must be deliberate, systematic, and consistent." That's why it's vital that your church's mission, vision, values, purposes, and personality are all communicated accurately in your printed material.

One Story, Many Ministries

Although you don't want to tell your church's *entire* story in every individual piece, you do want your guests to recognize that there is *one* story. Often a local church's message gets diluted because every ministry in the church is operating on its own without really collaborating with other ministries. When this happens, the church's overall mission is lost on its guests.

> Often a local church's message gets diluted because every ministry in the church is operating on its own without really collaborating with other ministries.

I visited a church in Michigan and found an oversized missions-outreach brochure at an information kiosk. Printed on glossy card stock with full-color, high-resolution artwork, it was definitely the classiest piece on display. By comparison, small-group ministries, children's ministries, and the weekend program were all printed in grayscale on various colors of paper. This disparity communicated one of two things to me, a guest.

First, I wondered if the church had corporately agreed that this was the predominant message it wanted to convey. Did it intend to draw attention to this piece at the expense of the other ministries? If this was the case, the goal had been accomplished.

My second theory was likely the more accurate one. Perhaps this church had not decided to publicize all its ministries through one communication channel, thereby telling one consistent story with one consistent voice. It appeared that the missions department had landed its own marketing-savvy team member who had resourcefully utilized funds to produce a smart, captivating brochure to communicate *that department's* message. As worthy as missions are, this church may need to reconsider how to best communicate its corporate message.

Every ministry within your local church should exist to advance the mission and vision of your church's corporate ministry. Find the communications experts within your body who will bring synergy to your logo, weekend program, and other printed messages. Don't allow ministries to compete for attention; this will only result in uncertainty about your church's priorities.

Don't allow ministries to compete for attention; this will only result in uncertainty about your church's priorities.

If you have ministries that appear to be competing, there may be confusion over who exists to support whom. If you have a ministry that assumes the church exists to support and help promote it, you'll need to resolve mission and alignment issues. These larger issues will not be corrected by a communications-team strategy.

Corporately determine your mission, articulate your vision, align every ministry, and commission them all to advance this one mission and vision. Then prioritize and synergize. What part or parts of the story will you spotlight in this season, during this month, or on this weekend? Guide your communications team to serve each ministry while keeping the church's priorities in mind. Tell one clear story with one clear voice.

What's Important to Them Is More Important Than What's Important to You

Create printed materials with your readers in mind. If you're printing materials targeted at your weekend crowd, then focus on first-time, new-to-church guests.

What about your mission and vision do these guests care about? What are their interests and needs? What do they want to know? What will help them feel safe in your church and encourage them to return? How will you ensure that your written communications don't keep your guests at arm's length? How should your content and vocabulary change to connect with your guests as well as with your members?

Paul talks about this: "Each of you should look not only to your own interests, but also to the interests of others" (Philippians 2:4). Paul is writing about our tendency to not see past our own noses. Then, as he prepares to paint a picture of the model of Christ, who looked past his own rights and interests because of his love for us, he writes, "Your attitude should be the same as that of Christ Jesus" (verse 5). This truth needs to be applied to all our relationships, including our relationships with our guests.

On a visit to another church, I picked up brochures on missions, small groups, care ministries, and membership. I read the material to understand what the service didn't fully tell me about the church. Because I was reading it for the first time, I noticed typos, poorly organized information, and—most of all—how little of it mattered to me as a guest.

Invite, Don't Exclude

In all of your communications, be careful to avoid churchy language that may cause guests to feel excluded. We don't intend church to be a club, but if certain words, information, and codes are needed to get in, that's the message we've inadvertently conveyed. Jesus called this *religion* and had some harsh comments about it.

The Message renders Jesus' words in Matthew 9:13 this way: "Go figure out what this Scripture means: 'I'm after mercy, not religion. I'm here to invite outsiders, not coddle insiders.' " Jesus invites those who are outside the holy huddle to cross the welcome mat and discover real life in him. Consider his words in Matthew 11:28: "Are you tired? Worn out? Burned out on religion? Come to me. Get away with me and you'll recover your life. I'll show you how to take a real rest" (The Message). Invite people inside. Avoid language that suggests an inside track is required to understand or participate.

> *Jesus invites those who are outside the holy huddle to cross the welcome mat and discover real life in him.*

Consider specific words used in many churches, such as *study, mature, the world, ecumenical, narthex, disciple*, and *omniscient*. Do these words help guests connect, or do they alienate them? Does your church use language that reopens the wounds of guests who were burned by former church experiences?

In writing for your church, choose common, cultural language that people understand. I suggest writing as though doing so for a mall newsletter or community newspaper. This doesn't mean you should remove any reference to God, church, or your mission. The point is to write simply, with your guests in mind.

Quality Doesn't Mean *Expensive*

Strive for excellence in all of your written communications. Guests may question the value you place on them or on your own ministry if your printed communication is sloppy, full of typos, and ambiguous. However, excellent printed materials do not have to be expensive. A weekend bulletin may be printed in grayscale or black ink on white paper and be excellent. Quality does not require color or heft. When care is taken to produce typo-free, legible print with plenty of white space, guests and members alike will be free of distractions and invited into the life and purpose of the church. And that really is the point, isn't it?

The Power of the Printed Program

Take a look at last week's bulletin or program. Using an M for "member" and a G for "guest," indicate the intended audience for each item. OK, you can mark a B for "both"; that's likely to be the case quite often. Include graphics, even the image supplied by the bulletin printer.

Now review the items you marked with a G or a B. Did you mark the financial information? Did you mark the board meeting reminder? What about the report on how many attended Jane's baby shower last week? Then consider carefully whether your guests really want to know things that you think are important.

What is your guests' interest in attendance figures or the year-to-date budget and financial-giving statement? Maybe they actually do care. But have you considered *why* these items are in your weekend printed material? Are they there for members, who could get the information elsewhere? Are they a help or distraction for your guests?

Is there anything in the weekend program or bulletin that in any way causes guests to feel as though they don't belong? Is there anything that communicates, "This is a closed community with its own inside information"? I'm not suggesting that important matters such as growth tracks shouldn't be communicated; I'm just urging you to consider *how* they are communicated.

Review your M, G, and B markings one more time. Do member-specific notations predominate? Give a bulletin to a friend who doesn't attend your church, and ask him or her to help you evaluate its usefulness to guests.

Remember, one of the primary questions guests are asking is "Do I fit here?" followed closely by "Does this church offer anything I need?" How do your printed communications align with your mission and help answer these two questions?

How would your printed program look if you tried to include basic information that helps guests connect meaningfully with God and with people? Answering the following questions may help you make your guests your first priority:

- **What's happening today? What can our guests expect in the service?** It may be helpful for your guests to see at least a brief outline of the service so they know how the service will unfold. They may appreciate knowing when to expect the end of the service or who the soloist is. Consider your culture and your guests' expectations. In the end you may choose not to include this kind of information, or you may choose to list the order of the entire service.

"What's happening today?" isn't limited to the service. For instance, you could include a paragraph about the purpose of the children's center. By doing so, you convey the value placed both on the children and on clear communication with their parents.

Consider outlining the intent of the offering. For a very long time, the issue of money and the church has been a barrier for people checking out the claims of Christ. We work hard to restrict our call for tithes and offerings to those who have said, "I'm following Jesus with my whole life here, with this group of believers." Our guests are not expected to give at all. Make it clear both from the platform and in the bulletin that the offering does not come from guests; it is from members and regular attendees.

While guests are on campus, there are many opportunities for them to engage in community and take other next steps. We have anticipated questions about other service times, our restaurant, the bookstore, and prayer needs. All of this and more are referenced in our printed program.

- **Who are we as a church?** People care about a church's roots, history, and track record. Guests want to know what you intend to do, why you are doing it, and how you will get it done. Provide a brief history of your church, telling guests how things got started and who has been involved. A brief glance at the past will help guests to connect with your vision for the future.

Your mission clarifies why your church exists. Ensure that your mission statement contains words your guests can easily understand. Make sure nothing in the mission statement will cause people to feel like objects, a target to be hit. Remember to invite, rather than exclude, your guests. For example, in our mission statement we've avoided words such as *disciple* and *discipleship* because these words require explanation. Our mission statement is simple: "Helping people take their next step toward Christ...together."

A brief description of your church's vision, primary purposes, and core values is also critical to help your guests understand its identity, how it does ministry, and where it

Guests who have not been part of your history need a picture of the future; it is the one concept they can share with everyone else at your church.

is headed. Guests who have not been part of your history need a picture of the future; it is the one concept they can share with everyone else at your church.

- **How do people connect?** Your guests want to know how they can *belong*. Within the Granger program, guests are directed to easily accessible on-ramps to connect. Opportunities to serve and grow are listed, along with web links. Every program outlines one or more ways to take a next step.

Signage

Your most prominent sign is probably the one facing the street; more than any other piece, it tells the community who you are. Think carefully about its message, particularly if it announces more than your church's name.

For example, what might people read between the lines of a simple statement such as "Visitors welcome"? To many, the term *visitor* suggests outsider. Visitors are considered one-timers, with little likelihood of ever belonging. In my opinion, when churches use this term, they risk conveying that they're OK with this arrangement. On the other hand, the term *guest* suggests honor. An invitation has been offered.

If you're using the term *visitor* anywhere, in either spoken or written communications, I urge you to drop it from your vocabulary.

What other messages does your street sign convey to your community and to potential guests? I've seen all kinds of messages on church reader boards. What do you suppose these statements say to people who haven't attended the local church?

"The wages of sin is death; repent before payday."

"Join us to battle against truth decay."

"Friends don't let friends go to hell."

Without realizing it, too many churches have earned an identity based on what they are against, rather than what they're for. I wonder if some churches intending to *hold the line* on sin aren't actually *drawing a line* for those outside the church. I fear that too often it's a line that those we're trying to reach won't cross.

It's a heartbreaker that many passers-by find themselves on the other side of the line, ostracized, thinking they are the ones against whom the church stands.

Our Lord is about life. He is about people. People matter to God; therefore, they *must* matter to us. Read your signs again. Make sure they do not say "Don't you wish you were like us?" Instead, let those who pass your building every day read "Welcome!"

I wonder if some churches intending to *hold the line* on sin aren't actually *drawing a line* for those outside the church.

Signs: Beyond Direction

In 2012 we more than doubled our atrium/connection space at our Granger campus, creating new entry points, a new guest services center, a new restaurant, and a new bookstore. Part of our expansion included a sign audit, evaluating signage for our existing space as well as new placement of signs in the new areas.

We've discovered that guests care about three primary places when they enter a church building: Where do I go for the service? Where do my kids go? And where, oh where, is the restroom? We want people to find these places quickly and easily. So we've made sure those signs are prominent—impossible to miss.

It's also true that many people wish to not ask for help. They want to find a sign and make their own way. Consider the number of people who prefer to use self-serve features at gas stations, self-checkout lanes at grocery stores, and automated systems at banks. Sometimes it's more comfortable to avoid engaging a stranger for help. We'd rather do it on our own.

So our signs are big. Huge, actually. They are printed in easy-to-read fonts in colors that don't easily blend with the wall paint and other décor. People read signs on the move, as they're walking. Small, squiggly fonts might have character, but they're annoying to a guest wanting to find the restroom quickly.

Our signage overall also includes wall and window treatments displaying our mission and core values. Who we are is printed throughout our signage.

Signage is a great opportunity to communicate your church's identity *and* create an experience for your guests. Contract with professionals who understand printed communication, especially large signs. We have found groups such as Plain Joe Studies (plainjoestudios.com) to be invaluable partners. Working with the same group on more than one project builds partnerships that develop understanding of ministry philosophy and a result that is uniquely "you."

But don't let your budget stand in your way. People in your community and probably in your church can help you communicate well with your guests. Don't wait until you can do all you want to do. Get started today.

Try These Next Steps...

- Who is responsible for signage, banners, printed programs, and promotion pieces at your church? What is the connection between these people? What could be done to coordinate and synergize their efforts?

- Who is the audience for your weekend printed program or bulletin? Who is it really written for? How should the style or content of your printed pieces be altered so your guests feel included?

Endnotes

1. Jesper Kunde, *Corporate Religion* (London: Pearson Education Limited, 2000), 59.

2. Maurilio Amorim, "Church Branding or Marketing? What's the Difference?" http://www.maurilioamorim.com/2011/04/church-branding-or-marketing-whats-the-difference/

9

Beyond the Weekend

> *"If you have to ask the question 'Why should we try to make it great? Isn't success enough?' then you're probably engaged in the wrong line of work."* [1]

First Impressions Matter All Week Long

Some time ago I phoned an Italian restaurant my wife and I had not yet tried, to confirm its hours and coupon acceptance. (Yeah, I'm that cheap!) When the phone was finally answered, the gruff voice on the other end simply said "Hello." I had to ask if this was the restaurant I had intended to call. He assured me it was and added, "We're not open on Mondays." That was it. No offer of help. No mention of dining hours the rest of the week. The conversation was over. He was finished.

And so was I.

Your guests are aware of you before they ever arrive on your campus. First impressions are being made all week long, whether you know it or not. People can be dissuaded from visiting your church before they ever set foot in the building. If a telephone receptionist is curt, a building is visibly deteriorating, or an advertisement is misspelled, a potential guest may very well choose to explore no further.

Consider for a moment the various points of contact potential guests have with your church before they ever attend a weekend service:

- your church property
- phone listing
- newspaper advertisement

- website

- neighborhood mailings

- staff interactions when receiving deliveries

- word-of-mouth reports from guests who attended last weekend

All these points of contact influence potential guests. Will those impressions draw them to your church or cause them to stay away?

Who's Answering the Phone?

When people responsible for answering their organization's phone consider it a distraction, callers know it. Remember the rule of representation? When callers talk to your church's receptionist, as far as they're concerned, they're talking to your church. Like it or not, what your guests think of your receptionist is what they think of your church.

So who's answering your church's phone during the week? Your guests can quickly answer the following questions for you; I encourage you to answer them first:

- Is your receptionist *SHAPEd* for the phone? Does his or her unique wiring fit this role?

- Is he or she characterized by any of these words: *warm, cheerful, inviting, accommodating, resourceful, focused?*

- What else are you asking your receptionist to do? Does the workload prevent him or her from answering the phone with warmth and genuine attention?

- Is the receptionist well-informed, with a working system to connect callers with your staff?

Your receptionist should convey over the telephone the same warmth and sense of welcome that you want your guests to experience on the weekend. At Granger we want our guests to experience an atmosphere of friendliness and caring; we want them to know we value them. Once you determine the experience you desire for your weekend guests, be sure to create it during the week as well.

The Dreaded "Will You Hold, Please?"

Most of the time, the receptionist's job is to route the caller to someone else. What happens after a caller to your church hears "One moment, please"? How long is the wait? What does the caller hear while waiting? This waiting time can make an impression that lasts long after the phone call.

Music can enhance an on-hold experience, if only for a few seconds. Great music can even provide an enjoyable few seconds. The music should be consistent with your church's personality. If music by Maranatha! helps define your church's identity, you should play it. Play music that reflects the weekend experience. At Granger we don't play the music as loudly on our phone lines as we do in the weekend services, but the music reflects our culture. Whatever music is playing, the guest should never hear a full song. That's a 3- to 4-minute wait. Generally people hang up after a minute or so.

Many people in your church don't know what goes on in the day of a pastor or church staff member. People tend to have a rather limited and distorted view of our daily responsibilities. I've actually been asked, "So what do you do all week?" The question is innocent. Many people in your congregation think church happens on the weekend and that during the week church staffers sit by the phone, waiting for the next call for help. Obviously, this is a misperception, but it is widely held, and your receptionist must be prepared to deal with it.

If the staff person is not available, your system should easily provide a voicemail system or a secondary contact. When your receptionist doesn't know what to tell the caller about your whereabouts, he or she is embarrassed, and the caller correctly assumes there's little communication within the church.

Voicemail That Makes You Smile

Automated, computer-generated messages are customer enhancements from phone and support services, but what offers us increased efficiency and productivity isn't necessarily all that helpful to our guests. In this fast-paced, "get it done yesterday" culture, people still tend to bristle at a computerized voice announcing, "The person you are calling is unavailable. Please leave a message at the tone." To avoid this, be sure to record your own voicemail message.

Remember, your guests' encounter with one individual is their experience with your church. You are your church, in person or on the phone. What will people think or feel as a result of hearing your voicemail? Here are some things to consider as you prepare your outgoing announcement:

- Imagine the faces of your potential callers: your guests, your members, the person you most respect, your mother. Plan to record your message as if they were all listening.

- Write your message before recording it. Take the time to wordsmith.

- Chew a large spoonful of peanut butter. Just kidding. Don't chew anything.

- Include your name, when the caller can expect to hear from you, and alternate ways to get help, such as through an assistant or a receptionist.

- Stand up and smile as you record your message. Your smile will come through your voice. Most voicemail messages sound lifeless and boring. Don't let yours sound like you're sick or hate what you're doing. And avoid recording when you have a sinus infection.

- Record in a quiet place. No one wants to hear honking horns as you're commuting to the church office.

- Listen to your message. If you were the caller, would you want to hear this?

- Record it again. Record until you get it right. Hear the smile. Feel the warmth.

- You're not finished. Keep your message current, updating it daily if necessary.

Always Return Calls Promptly

First impressions will be forgotten when the last or most recent impression overwhelms the initial experience. Let's say a guest (who has not been to your campus yet) calls you for information and is pleased with your velvet-voiced receptionist, who efficiently delivers the call to your direct line. Unfortunately, you are out and the guest gets your voicemail. Even so, you've carefully scripted your announcement, and your guest is impressed with how personable you sound over the phone. She looks forward to connecting with you. So far she is pleased.

Then she waits. A full day passes. No call. She understands; you're busy. Certainly she's not the only person who called you yesterday. She'll give you some grace. Two days and no call. But it's early in the day; there's still time. By that evening she realizes it's been two days, and she hasn't heard a word from you. By day three she's concluding she may have to call you back. Now she's annoyed. The initial impression from a few days ago is gone. The lasting impression is negative. This experience alone will help your guest decide if she will seek any further contact with your church.

Sound far-fetched? Not from my experience. In fact, a couple of poorly timed return calls from me ended in just this manner. Yes, the pace is fast. Yes, the role often demands more than can be done in a day. This is why a system to help you return calls promptly is so critical. I don't know of a one-size-fits-all system that works for everyone. Experiment with some of these ideas:

- Build in accountability. On your voicemail announcement, tell your callers when they can expect to hear from you, then stick to it. Better yet, commit to returning the call within 24 hours, unless you're gone for an extended period of time.

- Set aside a period of time each day to return phone calls.

- If you have an assistant, have him or her retrieve your messages once or twice a day and deliver them to you. If you can delegate calls to your assistant, do so.

The Old Church Van and Other Signs of Death

Several years ago one of my colleagues and I were headed to Chicago for a conference. He's an expert at finding great rates online. This time he had secured a hotel name, an address, and a great rate. We turned onto the street of the hotel. This was an upscale, classy area; what a bargain! But our excitement dwindled as we watched the high-rise hotels disappear in the rearview mirror. Within just a few minutes we looked at each other and said, "We aren't in Kansas anymore."

> The period of time a guest experiences between one point of contact and the next is white space. It is space waiting to be filled.

We had entered an industrial zone of smog and single-story buildings. The distance from the conference site was growing, and our hope for acceptable accommodations was diminishing. When the hotel finally came into view, its chipped paint, paper notices taped all over the glass, and the absence of cars in the parking lot told us all we needed to know without ever stepping inside.

What does your church property tell people about your church? Is the church van from 1972 (now a rimless rust bucket) still sitting as a monument to the Sunday school busing program that ended in 1978? Get rid of it. What about the chipping paint on the side of the building? Put together a work team to scrape it off and apply a new coat of paint. Are the weeds pulled? Is the lawn manicured? Are the trees pruned?

The bottom-line question when surveying your property is this: Does it look like anyone cares?

Everybody Smile! Your Church on the Worldwide Web

At any time of the day, any day of the week, people can access your church through your website. Your answering machine doesn't have to be on; your receptionist doesn't have to be in. For a growing number of people, this will be their first contact with your church. So two things are vital. First, your site must represent who you are. This is a great medium to reinforce your unique brand. Vision can be cast online in a compelling and engaging way. Is your church's personality clearly reflected on your website's home page?

For more information on establishing or enhancing your Web capabilities, visit the good folks at AspireOne (aspireone.com). This company provides churches as well as business strategic identity and communication solutions.

Second, your website should be a source of connection and ministry opportunities. Allow your guests and members to log on to the site and find ways to meet others and serve. A website that is merely an online billboard will not keep surfers or congregants on your domain for long. Your website should provide a source of connection, conversation, and other interactions.

Consider the potential for not only identifying your church online but also meeting your guests and members there. Go where people are, and communicate in a language that meets them physically, technologically, and relationally.

Ultimately, your online presence makes great stewardship sense. Your church can be quickly responsive to the culture, your community, the needs of your people, and the changing ministries of your church without incurring the costs of printing and mailing additional literature.

Your initial website launch doesn't have to include streaming media or messages. The important step is the first one: Get started. The online capabilities are limited only by the creativity of your team or a contracted support team. The same questions you ask in developing a relevant, guest-focused weekend printed program will help you get started in Web development: "What's happening?" "Who are we as a church?" and "How do guests connect?"

Coloring in the White Space

Imagine your spouse or very good friend has a birthday just around the corner. You want to honor this particular person with a nice dining experience at a local restaurant. The special day falls on a busy weekend for restaurants, so you call a month ahead to make reservations. It's all set. Your reservation is for 7 p.m. on Saturday, exactly four weeks out.

Advance the calendar three weeks; it's now seven days before the special evening. The phone rings. It's the maitre d' calling from the restaurant about your reservation. "Just my luck!" you think. "They've overbooked. They're probably going to bump me to 9 p.m.!"

"Mr. Waltz, I see you will be dining with us this Saturday evening. I'm calling to confirm your reservation."

"Yes, thank you. We're planning on 7 p.m. Does that still work?"

"Oh, yes. I wanted to see if you have any further requests. I can seat you and your party near the fireplace in our main atrium, or I have a table overlooking the lake in the east wing. Do you have a preference?"

"I'd love the window overlooking the lake, please. That's great. Thanks so much!"

"I have you down for a party of five. Is there a special occasion you're celebrating? And shall we plan for more than five?"

"No, still five. Actually, we're celebrating my wife's birthday."

"That's great, Mr. Waltz. We look forward to helping you celebrate. We'll anticipate seeing you for dinner at 7 p.m. next Saturday."

The period of time a guest experiences between one point of contact and the next is *white space*. It is space waiting to be filled. Nothing's happening. And nothing has to happen, but it could. This is "Wow!" territory.

White space is full of potential for the church. For example, when guests attend for the first time and they provide their e-mail or home address (voluntarily saying, "I'm here"), send them a letter or e-mail of welcome. Before your guests return for the next service, you've taken a step to acknowledge and welcome them. Fill in the white space.

When guests visit your website and make a request or ask questions, immediately generate an e-mail acknowledging their inquiries and promising to reply within 48 hours. That's filling the white space. When guests or members register for one of your classes, send them a postcard or e-mail, anticipating the day together and reminding them of times and any materials they'll need to bring.

There are countless other ways for church ministries to fill the white space:

- Send a confirmation letter, providing further information about an event.
- Place a phone call, inquiring about special needs at an upcoming retreat.
- Send a welcome letter with information about opportunities to connect.
- Provide a welcome packet for those who are new to your weekend service.
- E-mail the first night's lesson to new small-group members.

- Place a follow-up call to guests who had questions at the guest services center.

- Send additional information related to guests' registrations. (For example, when parents are signing up children for an event, provide information about other children's ministry opportunities.)

Where is your white-space opportunity? How will you utilize the telephone, your website, letters, e-mails, and face-to-face contact to tell your guests and members that they matter?

Color in the white space.

There's No Downtime for First Impressions

The opportunity to create "Wow!" experiences for your guests exists almost constantly—in the white space, in the moment, and outside the box. First impressions last. And last impressions last. There *is* no downtime.

Your guests have expectations and needs. As you listen, you'll understand their needs and expectations. And if you're able to clearly identify their expectations, you can define the experience before the experience. When you do that well, people will say, "Wow! I'm impressed!" And it will happen within the first 10 minutes.

Let the "Wows" begin!

Try These Next Steps...

- What do you hear when you phone your church after office hours? During the workday? How easy is it to connect with someone who is helpful? What needs to be streamlined? What needs to be automated?

- What do people understand about your church when they drive by? What's being communicated that you don't want communicated?

- How can you creatively enhance your guests' experience by filling in the white space?

Endnote

1. Jim Collins, *Good to Great* (New York: HarperCollins Publishers Inc, 2001), 209.

10

Wow-Busters

"Well-spoken words bring satisfaction; well-done work has its own reward." (Proverbs 12:14, The Message)

What's Red and Blue and Confused All Over?

We've all battled with businesses over their policies. We've encountered rules that seemed antiquated, pointless, and bureaucratic. "I can't reverse that charge." "We don't sell the floor model." "I'm not authorized to give you that discount." And my favorite: "This is our policy." When rules are made for the convenience of the staff or the institution at the expense of the guest or customer, the tail is wagging the dog.

Years ago in the medical field there existed "red" rules and "blue" rules. Red rules are those that cannot be broken. On a hospital ward, one red rule is that a patient is not to receive any liquid or food unless the patient's chart authorizes it. Failure to follow this rule could threaten the patient's life or, at the very least, blow a scheduled test.

> **W**hen rules are made for the convenience of the staff or the institution at the expense of the guest or customer, the tail is wagging the dog.

Blue rules are those rules that are important because they help systems operate smoothly. These rules can be broken when necessary because breaking them does not create life-threatening situations. For example, allowing guests to visit a patient after visiting hours will probably cause the patient no harm.

Your Church's Weekend Rules

Make a list of the spoken and unspoken rules your church has established for the weekend services. Think of your parking lot, greeting ministry, children's ministry, telephones, restrooms, resources, guest services center, auditorium, and worship service itself. Check any of these that appear on your list:

___ No drinks in the auditorium.

___ No running in the halls.

___ Male staff members must wear ties.

___ Pastors must hold a Bible while preaching.

___ No parking at the curb.

___ Do not use this door.

___ This is not a public phone.

___ No smoking on church property.

What other rules made your list?

_____

_____

_____

Your church has policies and rules. Some of them are red rules; they are important for the safety of your guests and the integrity of your people. Others are blue rules; they keep operations running smoothly, but they can be broken with few or no consequences. But often we don't distinguish a blue rule from a red rule, and we treat all of them as if they're equally important.

Complete the exercise in the box to the left. Mark each of the rules on your list with an R (for "red rule: cannot be broken") or a B (for "blue rule: helps operations, but can be broken"). Scrutinize your list carefully. How many of these rules would cause serious damage if broken, and how many are really about ease and systems?

Here are some rules that initially appeared on our list at Granger:

- No food or drink, except bottled water, may be brought into the auditorium during services.

- Never point in order to direct a guest to a location.

- Never open the rear auditorium doors after a service has begun.

- No child may leave the children's center without a corresponding check-in tag in the guardian's hand.

- No one may park at the curb.

However, as we reviewed the list, we realized only one rule was really a red rule: "No child may leave the children's center without a corresponding check-in tag in the guardian's hand." The consequences for breaking this rule could be serious. It's red.

The rule we treat as red, although it's probably blue, is "Never point in order to direct a guest to a location." While breaking this rule is not dangerous, we haven't been able to think of a reason to ever break it.

Note this fact: If you don't distinguish a rule as red or blue, those enforcing the rule will almost always enforce it as a red rule. Here's a painful example.

When we first opened our auditorium in the spring of 2000, we had concern about maintaining our carpet and seats, given our current cleaning equipment. So we created a rule: no drinks in the auditorium, except bottled water. We didn't tell our teams it was a red rule, but we didn't tell them it was a blue rule either.

One Sunday morning I watched and listened as a guest attempted to take her mocha from our café into the auditorium.

Usher: "I'm sorry, we only allow bottled water in the auditorium."

Guest: "But I just purchased this."

Usher: "I'm sorry, only bottled water."

Guest: "But I bought it from your café. I have a lid. I just want to sit with my husband right there at the back."

Usher: "I'm sorry. Can I get you a water?"

I was horrified. Really. I hadn't communicated whether this was a red rule or a blue rule. We had trained the script this usher had used, but hearing it play out in real time only elevated the truth: It was a script. An unchangeable, intolerant script. Ugh.

Here's another blue rule that can go south if enforced as red: "Never open the rear auditorium doors after a service has begun." Our services are programmed with great artistic elements such as drama, music, and electronic media to engage people in the relevance of the message. Because of the special lighting used to support these elements, we intentionally didn't put handles on the exterior of the main auditorium doors. Guests arriving late are directed to side entrances where double doors prevent the hallway light from pouring into the room. We don't want a poignant moment to be lost for several hundred people because a shaft of light caused them to turn to see what was going on. During the service, ushers are posted inside at the center auditorium doors to direct people wishing to exit to the side doors.

However, when given a choice between a stream of light momentarily pouring into the room and helping a parent with a crying baby make a speedy exit through the center door, the choice is clear. As natural as crying is for a baby and as cute as his cooing is to his family, several hundred people have already been distracted by the child's behavior. Mom walks down the center aisle toward the rear door. Everybody's already looking at her, and they watch the usher block the exit and send the mom all the way around the room to the side entrance. Wouldn't it be less disruptive to just open the door wide enough to allow Mom and baby to slip out? It's a blue rule. It's an exception to break it, but ushers are empowered to make that call.

Confusion over red and blue rules is a certain wow-buster. Huddle your team together. Approach your conversation from the vantage point of safety and service. Then clarify what's red and what's blue. If you finish up with more red than blue, you probably still have some work to do.

Five Things You Don't Want to Hear From Your Team

1. "I Didn't Know I Was Serving Today."

As I've talked to churches about developing their guest services ministry, the most consistent question has been "How do I get people to show up?" Sometimes well-meaning folks will sign up and then never show up. Or many of those who do show up, show up late.

When people embrace a vision worth giving their lives to and they derive value from serving, they will show up and serve as to Christ. Beyond that, simple communication will ensure that every team member knows when he or she is expected to serve. Developing behind-the-scenes administrative teams and systems will help. Consider these ideas:

- Have an administrative person or team organize team rosters.

- Empower that same person or team to send an e-mail, mail reminder postcards, or call every week.

- Encourage team leaders to mail thank-you notes to their team members after serving over the weekend.

- Provide every team member with a schedule for the entire calendar year.

- Have team coaches encourage team members individually throughout the weekend, praising their specific efforts and unique contributions.

- Begin pre-service meetings on time. This will communicate the value of promptness in team members.

2. "What's Wrong With What I'm Wearing?"

Of course this question comes up on the spot, as your inappropriately dressed team member is greeting guests at the front door. People don't try to cross the lines; they often just don't know where the lines are. You cannot assume everyone shares your background, knowledge, or judgment. Again, upfront communication to everyone will minimize these surprises.

First, decide what is appropriate in your church culture. For several years we expected all our guest services teams to dress a notch above the crowd attending our services. For us this meant we expected no denim, no T-shirts, and no tennis shoes. We expected pressed clothing and shined shoes. Our people were professional in appearance and service.

Now, several years later, our culture has changed. We've always been very informal and casual at Granger, but years ago denim became the new business casual, and untucked shirts, tennis shoes, and flip flops are the norm. Our people dress in a variety of styles, indicative of the diversity of our weekend crowds.

We've always wanted our guests to see people like themselves when they arrive on campus. It's important to newcomers that they fit—in age, appearance, and interests. A more casual shoe is fine. We ask for only two things: authenticity and modesty.

To address the modesty question, we ask our team members to avoid wearing T-shirts promoting tobacco or alcohol or containing sexual innuendos. Also, as hip as they might be, we ask that they not wear jeans with holes in questionable areas. Nuff said. To female teammates we've said, "If a guest drops something and you bend to pick it up, people should still wonder." Women are expected to dress modestly, avoiding miniskirts, deep neckline plunges, and tightly fitting clothing that draws attention to themselves. The goal for each of us is to point people to Jesus, not to ourselves.

> The goal for each of us is to point people to Jesus, not to ourselves.

3. "You Don't Need Me."

Paul addresses this remark in 1 Corinthians 12:14-20:

> Now the body is not made up of one part but of many. If the foot should say, "Because I am not a hand, I do not belong to the body," it would not for that reason cease to be part of the body. And if the ear should say, "Because I am not an eye, I do not belong to the body," it would not for that reason cease to be part of the body. If the whole body were an eye, where would the sense of hearing be? If the whole body were an ear, where would the sense of smell be? But in fact God has arranged the parts in the body, every one of them, just as he wanted them to be. If they were all one part, where would the body be? As it is, there are many parts, but one body.

It's possible that team members who feel unnecessary simply need to be reassured of their value. They may be serving in an area where they don't see many people, yet their role is key to the individuals they serve. Perhaps they're serving behind the scenes, away from the energy of the ministry. These persons need to be reminded often of the vision they are helping to fulfill. This sense of value is best communicated relationally, as their team leaders become acquainted enough with them to understand their needs, personalities, and communication preferences. The reminder that every team member matters may be communicated orally or in writing, but the reminder must be given frequently and sincerely.

Sometimes people feel unnecessary because they aren't serving in the right place. I've heard Rick Warren say that one is never the wrong person; one may simply be in the wrong place. Once people find the right places to serve, they won't feel as if they aren't needed.

> **O**nce people find the right places to serve, they won't feel as if they aren't needed.

4. "Are We Finished Yet?"

This comment, whether expressed orally or in body language, reveals an underlying sentiment. Rather than confront the statement alone, the leader should try to understand what's below it. Team members who ask this question either have missed the vision of their roles, underestimate their own value to the ministry, or are in the wrong place. There is one other possibility: They may need to examine their hearts to be certain they are serving for unselfish reasons, rather than expecting to *be* served.

You might initiate a private conversation by asking, "What are you enjoying and not enjoying about this role?" or "How great is your sense of fulfillment in this role?" As these questions are answered, you'll likely begin to understand what this person needs: vision, value, a new venue for ministry, or a change of heart.

5. "They," "Them," and "You Guys"

This language reveals a great deal about alignment and ownership. Sometimes a newer person to the church will use these words when referring to the church or the ministry team. For the new person, it is often innocent and discloses nothing except newness. However, when used by the veteran member, these words often suggest an "outside the ministry" posture, a lack of alignment to the leadership or mission. This person may feel as if he or she would do much of the ministry differently, but "this is the way *they* want it done."

This language requires a conversation, and it should occur sooner rather than later. I would begin the conversation by assuming the person's language is unintentional and innocent. After affirming the person and the positive characteristics he or she brings to the ministry, the conversation might unfold as follows:

"Because we value trust in our serving relationships, I believe you'd want me to make observations that might help you improve your ministry. I've noticed from time to time that you refer to our church staff or pastors as 'they' or 'them.' It's probably quite unintentional, but I wanted to talk to you about it in case you have any concerns or questions."

If the team member indicates that he or she somehow feels "beneath" the leadership, you have an opportunity to illustrate his or her value by pointing out, "You *are* the church. You make this ministry happen. We're all in this together."

If, however, the team member expresses complaints or concerns about church leadership, then a conversation about those issues, appropriate ways to resolve conflict, the church's vision, and cooperative ownership is in order.

Five Things You Don't Want Your Guests to Hear From Your Team

1. "That's Not My Responsibility."

This comment may cause team members to feel as though they've covered themselves, but the guest doesn't care who is responsible. The guest merely wants the question answered or the request filled.

The risk of dropping the ball increases each time a request, question, or need is passed on to another person. This is true whether it's a form, a phone number, an e-mail, or a voicemail message. The person who hears a concern, is asked a question, or takes a request for information should be the one to follow it through to completion. In fact *because* he or she first heard the inquiry, he or she is responsible for answering it. When this happens, it is a guaranteed "Wow!" for the guest.

> The risk of dropping the ball increases each time a request, question, or need is passed on to another person.

Here's an example. A guest walked up to Debbie at the guest services center and asked a question about an online registration process he'd used a few days before. The problem wasn't anticipated, so the answer wasn't readily apparent. Debbie took the guest's name and contact info and promised to find the answer. She discovered the answer by the end of her shift on Sunday. Before the afternoon was over, Debbie called the guest and resolved the confusion.

The guest would have been happy to have the information from anyone, but Debbie's diligence and commitment told him he was dealing with a person, not an institution. Whether they ever speak again, Debbie has reinforced our church's core value of relational ministry in the mind of this guest and created a powerful "Wow!"

2. "I Don't Know."

If a team member doesn't have an answer, he or she must be resourceful enough to find it. It's OK not to know an answer; it's *not* OK to leave it there. The team member must take the initiative to *find* the answer.

Our responsibility as leaders is to anticipate as much as possible so we're able to inform our teams. Remember, information is empowering. Teams should also note frequently asked questions over the weekend, along with the answers they found. Making this information available fills in the gaps in future services or weeks. "I don't know" must always be followed by "but I'll find out."

> "I don't know" must always be followed by "but I'll find out."

3. "No."

Yeah, but, sometimes the answer *is* "no." Why would we not say "no" if the answer to the question is "no"? Simply because when you're the guest, you expect the answer to be "yes." You want to be satisfied. When you hear "no" without an alternative or an explanation, you're unsatisfied.

If we've done the work of distinguishing between red and blue rules, we've eliminated most opportunities to say "no." At the same time, saying "yes" every time, even in response to blue rules that are about flow and efficiency, *can* create problems. Consider these scenarios.

"May I take my coffee into the auditorium?"

Remember, for a while at Granger this was a blue rule. The easy answer was "No, we don't allow it." But it was a better response to reply "We prefer bottled water in the auditorium. May I get you some?" Better yet, breaking this rule was the step we determined and eliminated it all together.

In his book *Customer Satisfaction Is Worthless, Customer Loyalty Is Priceless,* Jeffrey Gitomer suggests we ask ourselves, "What would Grandma think?" If the answer we'd give Grandma isn't "No," "I can't," or "I don't want to," then we shouldn't respond to our guests that way either.[1] As compelling a figure as Grandma is, in the church we have an even better model. Jesus said, "Anything you did for any of my people here, you also did for me" (Matthew 25:40, New Century Version).

Even churches can get stuck in policy ruts. When tempted to say "no" or give the standard response, ask this question: "Would I say 'no' to my grandma or—better yet—to Jesus?"

4. "They," "Them," and "You Guys"

Everyone wants to appear competent. When we don't have the answers or the rule is difficult to explain, the temptation to blame someone else is tremendous. It can be difficult for people to recognize this temptation in themselves. But when the team member says, "They said" or "It's up to them" or "You guys had better," he or she is communicating a lack of ownership. When guests overhear this language or pick up on this attitude, they doubt the church itself.

5. "I'm Just a Volunteer."

I always ask sales associates or clerks, "How are you?"

It's amazing how many times they respond, "I'll be doin' much better when I can leave this place! Only two more hours to go."

I've not done this yet, but I'm sorely tempted to reply, "I feel as if I'm ruining your day. You think your job is punching in, standing all day, pressing buttons on a register, bagging food, and taking money. But the truth is, I'm your job! Making me happy to be here is your job. Thanking me for giving you my business so you can have a paycheck is your job."

Too many people are unhappy working day after day in the same grueling job. That should never happen in the church. Those who plug into a ministry should do so because they fully embrace its mission and vision. If they do, no one will ever hear these words from them.

To help ensure that your team members are serving in roles for which they are wired, use the assessment tool "Reviewing My SHAPE for Guest Services Ministry" on pages 141 and 142. It will help team members evaluate their own level of fulfillment and fun in serving on any of your guest services teams. Working through the SHAPE acronym will help them review each aspect of their serving makeup.

Break the Mold; Create the "Wow!"

Remember, creating the "Wow!" isn't about you. It is all about your guests. It's all about them coming back to your church so they can discover God's love.

First impressions really do matter. They matter on first dates, job interviews, and in the ministry of the local church. They're automatic and involuntary. You have the opportunity to influence the outcome of your guests' experience by deciding in advance what that experience will be.

Break the mold. There's always room for improvement.

People matter to God. Make sure they know they matter to your church, too. Create the "Wow!"

Try These Next Steps…

- What red rules should be changed to blue rules? How can you accomplish this?

- What wow-busters are you hearing from your people? What do you think is causing them? Is there vision leak? Is there a breakdown in communication? What can you do to repair the damage?

- Is there someone in your ministry with whom you need to meet regarding his or her alignment, fit, or character? How will you approach this conversation with grace so this person knows he or she is valued?

Endnotes

1. Jeffrey Gitomer, *Customer Satisfaction Is Worthless, Customer Loyalty Is Priceless* (Atlanta: Bard Press, 1998), 123.

2. Paul R. Timm, *50 Powerful Ideas You Can Use to Keep Your Customers* (Franklin Lakes, NJ: The Career Press, Inc., 2002), 19.

Reviewing My SHAPE for Guest Services Ministry

Name _____

The best way to contact me is_____

My guest services team is_____

My leader is _____

Understanding how God is using my SHAPE in this ministry role

■ The degree to which my **S**piritual gifts are being utilized:

NOT AT ALL	STILL CONFUSED, BUT I THINK SO	SEEING THEM USED SOMEWHAT	PLEASED WITH USE OF MY GIFTS	GREAT!

/-----0--------------------- 1 ------------------- 2 --------------------3--------------------- 4 -----/

■ The degree to which my **H**eart—my passion—is connected to this ministry role:

NOT AT ALL	STILL CONFUSED, BUT I THINK SO	SEEING IT CONNECTED SOMEWHAT	MINISTRY CLEARLY CONNECTED	GREAT!

/-----0--------------------- 1 -------------------- 2 --------------------3--------------------- 4 -----/

■ The degree to which my **A**bilities are being used:

NOT AT ALL	STILL CONFUSED, BUT I THINK SO	SEEING THEM USED SOMEWHAT	PLEASED WITH USE OF MY ABILITIES	GREAT!

/-----0--------------------- 1 ------------------- 2 --------------------3--------------------- 4 -----/

■ The degree to which my **P**ersonality is being expressed:

NOT AT ALL	STILL CONFUSED, BUT I THINK SO	EXPRESSING IT AT TIMES	EXPRESSING IT WELL	GREAT!

/-----0--------------------- 1 ------------------- 2 --------------------3--------------------- 4 -----/

■ The degree to which my **E**xperiences are having a positive influence:

NOT AT ALL	STILL CONFUSED, BUT I THINK SO	SEEING THEM USED SOMEWHAT	PLEASED WITH THE VALUE THEY BRING	GREAT!

/-----0-------------------- 1 ------------------- 2 --------------------3---------------------- 4 -----/

■ Overall, I'd say that my **SHAPE** is being expressed in this ministry role:

NOT AT ALL	STILL CONFUSED, BUT I THINK SO	SEEING IT USED SOMEWHAT	PLEASED	GREAT!

/-----0-------------------- 1 ------------------- 2 --------------------3---------------------- 4 -----/

If any of your answers was less than "Great!" please take a moment to reflect on the following possibilities:

• I need to explore a different ministry area, one that better fits my SHAPE. This is not about issues with ministry leadership or relationships.

• I need to find a different role within this ministry. I have passion for this ministry and believe it's the right area for me to serve in. Here's what else I'd love to explore within this ministry:

_____

• I believe other things besides SHAPE are affecting my attitude, my sense of "being present," my ability to "make their day," and my level of fun. Other things are preventing fulfillment (check any that apply):

❑ My spiritual journey needs attention. I need to seek God personally about my relationship with him.

❑ My relationships with family or friends are interfering with my ability to give what I want to this ministry right now.

❑ Issues with work, school, or other time demands are pulling me in directions that I'm not managing well in conjunction with this ministry role.

❑ I don't feel I've connected with people on this team the way I would like to.

❑ Other: _____

Sign me up to serve in the upcoming year in the guest services ministry!

❑ Yes ❑ No

Epilogue

Lasting Impressions

It was the end of another long, grueling day. The road trip alone was exhausting, and some of the executive team were thinking that this stop could be a mistake. The opposing party would be out in force—media, crowds, the whole deal. And they were dreading it. An out-of-the-way, quaint spot would have suited them fine for this final party banquet, but *he* wanted to go to the big city. He wanted to find a quiet room where they could enjoy an intimate evening in the bustling city.

So here they were, greeting the public, making a grand entrance, completing the rounds. It was as tiring as they had expected. Upon entering the city, he asked some members of his team to finalize the evening plans.

So the room was procured. They would eat in the big city.

Dinnertime came, and they all convened. Then a fight broke out.

No one had secured the valet staff, the serving crew, or the set-up/tear-down crew. They crammed themselves in the doorway, arguing over who would be first to be seated, who would take everyone's coats, who would serve the meal, who would do the dishes.

He just shook his head. He made his way through the arguing team and began taking their coats. Then he served the meal. The team began to fidget. This didn't feel right. Their argument over who was *not* going to serve had become an embarrassment. Then he began to clear the table.

When Jesus' disciples got to the room for dinner, they had actually forgotten to arrange for a servant to wash their dirty feet. Jesus made his way through, not to wash the dishes but to wash the disciples' feet.

Jesus said, "I tell you the truth, no servant is greater than his master, nor is a messenger greater than the one who sent him. Now that you know these things, you will be blessed if you do them" (John 13:16-17). I hear Jesus saying, "Follow me. Do it the way I do it. This is how you're great in my eyes. This is how you serve."

Before the first book about customer service was written, before any seminars on guest services were conducted, before the phrase *first impressions* was coined, Jesus gave us the model. It starts with a towel over our arm. It takes us to our knees in humility. It has us focusing on others, as servants.

This is an invitation to put your towel over your arm, humbly get on your knees, and focus on others. This ministry is first and foremost about serving. We have one goal: that our guests will see our Master and be drawn to him.

It's all about Jesus.